Delicious
Bundt Cakes

D1561138

Delicious Bundt Cakes

More Than 100 New Recipes for Timeless Favorites

Roxanne Wyss and Kathy Moore

Photographs by Staci Valentine

St. Martin's Griffin
New York

This book is dedicated to
our families, who have loved and encouraged
our business for more than thirty years.

www.stmartins.com

The authors occasionally refer to product brand names or list trademarks in the recipe ingredients
or recipe title, and these trademarks are owned by their respective brands. This is an independent
work and is not endorsed, sponsored, or authorized by those brand owners.

Photographs by Staci Valentine
Food Stylist: Alyse Sakai
Book design: Michelle McMillian

The Library of Congress Cataloging-in-Publication Data is available upon request.

ISBN 978-1-250-17004-0 (trade paperback)
ISBN 978-1-250-17005-7 (ebook)

Our books may be purchased in bulk for promotional, educational, or business use. Please contact
your local bookseller or the Macmillan Corporate and Premium Sales Department at
1-800-221-7945, extension 5442, or by email at MacmillanSpecialMarkets@macmillan.com.

First Edition: September 2018

10 9 8 7 6 5 4 3

Contents

Chocolate Bundt Cakes

Pound and Coffee Cakes

Marbles, Tunnels, Swirls, and Filled Bundt Cakes

A Year of Bundts

Glazes, Frostings, and Fillings

Introduction

Does a gorgeous Bundt cake make your eyes dance? These rich, buttery, totally irresistible cakes stand alone as a tribute to all things timeless and delectable. Bundt cakes are baked in every imaginable flavor, and they are now as trendy as the latest Instagram post or the new corner Bundt cake bakery. The recipes in *Delicious Bundt Cakes* make it easy to be a master baker. Enduring classics, fun retro recipes, luscious treats, and new flavor creations mean there is a flavor for everyone. Some recipes begin with cake mixes, while others begin with a few basic ingredients so you can find the perfect recipe for you.

The natural, photo-ready beauty of a Bundt cake means home cooks don't have to be a pastry chef or skilled cake decorator to create a masterpiece. No need to pull out the piping bags and cake decorating tips—the stellar design is baked right in.

A beautiful cake that is packed with real old-fashioned goodness and is easy to prepare! So what are you waiting for? Let's get started.

The Pan

What is a Bundt cake? It is a ring-shaped cake that is baked in a fluted tube pan.

The pan evolved from a traditional German pan and was introduced in the United States by Northland Aluminum, better known as Nordic Ware. The first and still classic Bundt pan is a fluted, ring-shaped pan manufactured by Nordic Ware. Today, the company offers several shapes and sizes of Bundt pans, and they continue to introduce new and unique Bundt pans each year. Other companies now offer ring-shaped baking pans, too (these won't be labeled "Bundt," but they can be used in place of a trademarked Bundt pan as long as the size and shape match).

Current pans are especially fun to use due to the variety of designs available. You can use ring-shaped pans with deep swirls or diamonds, intricate designs, or seasonal motifs.

Bundt cakes are the perfect cake for a beginning baker. The hole in the middle of the pan means the cake bakes more evenly. You won't find a soggy, underdone center like you might in a sheet or layer cake.

With so many shapes and looks, how do you choose which to use?

Material

Classic Bundt pans are cast aluminum so the sides are thicker. Yes, we know there are now various metal and even silicone pans, but we prefer the cast-aluminum ones. They bake more evenly, and we find that silicone pans can sometimes distort the shape of the cake. Lodge Manufacturing Company has introduced a cast-iron fluted cake pan. Cast iron, while heavy, bakes evenly and the iron will create a natural, easy-release finish over time. The recipes in this book were all tested in nonstick-coated, cast-aluminum pans.

Finish

The nonstick coating helps to keep the cakes from sticking, and when we buy pans, we choose those with a nonstick finish. Pans that are darker in color may result in a cake with a slightly thicker, darker crust, but only baking geeks like us will notice this.

Sizes

Bundt pans now range in size from large 15-cup pans to decorative 10- to 12-cup pans to individual or cupcake size.

The standard for listing a pan's volume is to measure the number of cups of water it holds when filled to the brim (so a 12-cup pan will hold 12 cups of water). This is not the number of cups of batter that will fit into the pan, as the cake batter will rise as it bakes. If you don't know the size of your pan, set the pan flat on the counter. Fill a liquid measuring cup with water and carefully pour the water into the pan, filling it until it nearly overflows and counting the cups as you go.

The recipes state the pan size, so you will know if a particular recipe is best baked in a 10-cup Bundt pan or if it requires a 15-cup Bundt pan.

If you must adapt a recipe to the pan you own, generally fill a Bundt pan no more than about three-quarters full. If in doubt, set the filled pan on a rimmed baking sheet to catch any overflow while baking.

Typically, if you own a 12-cup pan and choose a recipe that requires a 10-cup pan, it will be fine, as you can always use a larger pan than the one stated in the recipe.

Of course, it just stands to reason that trying to use a pan smaller than the one listed may pose a problem. To prevent cake batter from overflowing you will have to take some of the batter out. It is up to you if you choose to discard it or use it to bake a couple of cupcakes. If cupcakes are your way to go, spray the wells of a muffin pan with nonstick baking spray with flour, then spoon in the batter. Bake the cupcakes at 350°F for about 15 minutes, then begin checking for doneness.

Using pans of different sizes and shapes will affect the baking time. It is wise to check the baking progress about 5 minutes before the stated time, then monitor it closely until the cake tests done.

Sticking

Everyone at some time has experienced a cake—or two—sticking to the pan to ruin the look. We have all been there. But you can follow some easy tips to get that picture-perfect cake.

Before filling the pan with cake batter, spray the pan with nonstick baking spray with flour. Be sure to spray it evenly and cover all the crevices and points. Some manufactures void the warranty if nonstick cooking spray is used on the pan, especially if the pan is nonstick coated. Check with the manufacturer of your pan to confirm and follow their directions. Some

companies differentiate between cooking sprays with flour (which may be acceptable to use) and cooking sprays without flour (which are not recommended.)

Does a baking spray not appeal to you? To make your own special pan grease, in a food processor fitted with a metal chopping blade, combine ½ cup vegetable oil, ½ cup (1 stick) unsalted butter, and ½ cup all-purpose flour. Process until it forms a smooth paste. Spoon the grease into a jar with a tight-fitting lid or bowl with a tight-fitting cover. Store the grease in the refrigerator for up to a few months. To use it, spread the paste evenly over the inside of the pan using a folded paper towel, taking care to grease the crevices and points.

Be sure to start with a clean pan and coat it thoroughly. If there is residue on the pan from past baking endeavors, it will increase the likelihood of sticking.

If the cake you are making has a streusel filling or a sweet, creamy tunnel, try to keep the filling away from the sides of the pan, as it can sometimes increase the likelihood of sticking.

Even those pans that are nonstick coated should be greased or sprayed with nonstick baking spray with flour each time you use them.

After baking, let the cake cool a little—but not too long. Set the baked cake in the pan on a wire rack to cool for 10 minutes, then invert the cake and remove the pan. If you try to remove the hot cake from the pan too quickly, the cake will likely break apart, but if you let it cool completely, the cake will probably stick.

Is the Cake Done?

Bake the cake for the recommended time. Since ovens and the pan you use may vary from ours, the baking time is an estimate. Check for doneness during the last 5 minutes of baking, then monitor it closely so it is perfectly baked.

To test if the cake is done, insert a wooden pick into the center of the cake; the cake is done if it comes out clean. If the cake is not done, return it to the oven and bake for 2 or 3 minutes, or until it tests done.

For Bundt cakes, a longer wooden pick is the most convenient to use, but if you don't have one, use a piece of dry spaghetti. It will work perfectly.

If the cake has a tunnel of cream cheese or other unique filling inside, inserting a wooden pick into the center is not an accurate way to check for doneness. Other tests for doneness include checking to see if the sides of the cake begin to pull away from the sides of the pan or if the top springs back when lightly touched.

Glazing, Frosting, and Poking with Added Flavor

Once out of the pan, most Bundt cakes are cooled completely before being glazed or frosted.

Drizzling with a glaze is easy—so much easier than trying to frost a layer cake. And many Bundt cakes are so tasty that they don't need frosting or a glaze; just dust the cake with confectioners' sugar for a stellar look and flavor.

To make cleanup easy and to catch any drippings from the glaze, invert the cake onto a wire rack placed over a sheet of parchment paper, waxed paper, or aluminum foil.

Occasionally we recommend drizzling or brushing on a glaze while the cake is still warm; just follow the recipe recommendations.

For some glazes, we suggest poking small holes over the cake so the glaze can seep into the cake and add flavor to every bite. Sometime recipes will recommend using the tines of a fork for poking the holes, and that is fine, but our favorite tool to poke holes in a Bundt cake is a skewer. It will make a small hole that is just perfect for this cake.

Care and Cleaning of the Bundt Pan

Most Bundt pans are not recommended for the dishwasher, but don't let that scare you. Usually a quick wash with soap and hot water is all they need.

When using decorative Bundt pans (especially those with more intricate designs), you may want to use a soft brush to make cleanup easier. We find that a new toothbrush marked for this task is perfect.

Tips for the Best Results

Follow the recipes, using the ingredients listed. Substituting other ingredients, especially those labeled "low-fat" or "light," or ingredients formulated for special diets or to avoid specific allergens, may affect the results.

Spray the pan evenly with nonstick baking spray with flour.

Assemble all the ingredients before beginning. For the best results, the butter should be softened (i.e., left to stand at room temperature for about 30 minutes or until softened to the touch), and ingredients such as eggs, milk, and sour cream should be at room temperature.

Mix the cake according to the recipe. Adjust the racks in the oven so the Bundt cake will bake in the center of the oven, then preheat the oven to the temperature specified in the recipe. Use hot pad holders and be cautious, as the cake and oven are hot. Bake until the cake tests done, but try to avoid overbaking, as an overdone cake will taste dry.

Once out of the oven, set the pan on a wire rack. Set the timer to 10 minutes. When time is up, invert the cake onto the rack.

Store most baked Bundt cakes in a covered container at room temperature. Cakes with an egg-rich or cream cheese–filled tunnel or that have a cream cheese frosting need to be stored in the refrigerator.

Choose the Best Ingredients

Accurately measuring good-quality ingredients is the first step to the best baked goods. Baking is a precise science, so measure carefully.

Butter
Choose unsalted butter. We buy butter when we see it on sale. It can be frozen for up to 6 months.

Low-fat, light, soft, whipped, or tubs of butter all have different formulations than sticks of butter and are not recommend for these recipes, as the texture and the flavor of the baked cake will be adversely affected. For optimum flavor, we generally do not recommend using margarine.

Soften

Butter is "softened" when a slight indentation remains when touched lightly, yet the butter still holds its shape. You can set the butter out of the refrigerator for about 30 minutes, but don't let it sit out for several hours on a hot afternoon. Softened butter is best a little colder (ideally 65 to 70°F) than typical kitchens in the United States. If time is short and you forgot to set it out of the refrigerator or to quickly soften butter, you can cut the butter into pieces and place the pieces on a microwave-safe glass plate. Microwave on medium-low (20%) power for 10 to 15 seconds for 4 tablespoons (½ stick) butter or 20 to 25 seconds for 1 stick (½ cup) butter, until it just starts to soften. Let the butter stand for 10 minutes, then proceed with the recipe. Another tip to quickly soften butter is to grate the cold butter. Do not melt the butter unless the recipe specifies melted butter.

Cake Mixes

Many Bundt cake recipes begin with a cake mix.

Cake mixes are available in both double-layer- and single-layer-size packages. Cake mixes sized to make double-layer cakes are commonly used for Bundt cakes. Follow the recipe recommendation for the best results.

The package weight for many double-layer cake mixes ranges from 15.25 to 18 ounces, especially for common flavors such as yellow, chocolate, and vanilla. The national brands, including Betty Crocker, Pillsbury, and Duncan Hines, and many of the store brands generally seem to fall within this range, and this is the weight range we used to test these recipes. Some specific flavors range in weight from 16 to 19 ounces.

When selecting a cake mix, we recommend using one of approximately the same weight as listed in the recipe. The exact weight of the mix will vary

by brand and flavor, but we have found that the slight deviations do not affect the baking and still make great cakes.

Those cake mixes with pudding in the mix (often labeled "extra moist") and those without pudding work equally well. Use either type of cake mix for the recipes in this book. If the recipe you are using recommends to beat the cake mix with a pudding mix, and your cake mix lists that it already has pudding in it, go ahead and add in a separate package of pudding mix just as the recipe recommends.

Can you interchange flavors? Sure, but we recommend you choose a similar flavor for the best results. For example, if the recipe lists devil's food cake and you choose to use a chocolate cake mix, the recipe will work fine.

You will spot several brands of cake mix on the grocery store shelf; experiment a little to determine which you enjoy the most.

Stock up on cake mixes when they are on sale. Be sure to double-check the use-by date and use the cake mixes before they expire.

Chocolate

The array of baking chocolate has exploded, with many varieties, origins, and artisan products now available at the local grocery store. Common baking chocolate bars include unsweetened, semisweet, or bittersweet chocolate, while chips are now available in such flavors as semisweet and milk chocolate. Each variety has a slightly different flavor and level of sweetness, but we find that in our recipes you can generally substitute one variety of baking chocolate for another. Candy bars, on the other hand, are usually much sweeter, so we do not recommend substituting a chocolate candy bar for the baking chocolate. If a candy bar is to be used it is specified in the recipe.

Eggs

The recipes were tested using large eggs. Results will not be consistent if you use medium or jumbo eggs, or egg substitutes. For best results, use room-temperature eggs.

Flour

We recommend all-purpose flour for many recipes. To measure flour, spoon the flour out of the flour canister and into a dry measuring cup and then level it off with the flat edge of a butter knife or spatula. Do not dip the measuring cup into the flour canister or shake the cup to level it off. Flour does not need to be sifted for the recipes in this book.

Leavening Agents

Baking soda and baking powder are the chemicals that make cakes rise. Without them, the cake may be dense and heavy, but using a little baking soda or baking powder, or both, creates a light and wonderful cake. Baking soda reacts with acids, like vinegar, fruit juice, or buttermilk, while baking powder does not require an acid, so you will often see it used in cakes made with milk. Do not interchange baking powder with baking soda.

Milk and Other Liquids

Milk is often used in the recipes in this book. For optimum flavor, use regular whole dairy milk, but in a pinch, 2% or reduced-fat milk can be used. We love the tang of buttermilk. If you don't have buttermilk on hand, pour 1 tablespoon white vinegar or lemon juice into a 1-cup measuring cup and add milk to equal 1 cup. Allow it to stand for a few minutes, then measure out the volume you need for the recipe you are preparing.

Oil and Shortening

For baking, choose flavorless "neutral" oils, like canola, corn, or vegetable oil.

Vegetable shortening is solid at room temperature and essentially flavorless. To measure accurately, fill a dry measuring cup, pressing down to eliminate air pockets.

Salt

There is now an array of salt available—in different colors, origins, and textures. While we may turn to these for savory cooking, typical table salt is our choice for baking.

Sugars

Brown sugar is labeled dark or light, and you can use them interchangeably. The dark version has a more intense molasses flavor and is popular in Southern cooking. We find people often use the one they are most familiar with, frequently the one they grew up with—so Roxanne chooses dark and Kathy chooses light. Brown sugar is always measured "packed," so spoon it into the measuring cup and pack it lightly to eliminate air pockets; it should hold its shape when turned out into the mixing bowl.

To measure the granulated sugar called for in a recipe, fill a dry measuring cup to overflowing and then level it off with the flat edge of a butter knife or spatula.

These recipes were not tested with other sweeteners, and the use of alternative sweeteners may affect the results.

Nuts

Toasting pecans, walnuts, almonds, or other nuts intensifies their flavor. To toast nuts, spread them in a single layer on a rimmed baking sheet. Toast in the oven at 350°F for 5 to 7 minutes, or until lightly toasted.

Whipped Topping, Whipped Cream, or Ice Cream

You might enjoy a scoop of ice cream, or a dollop of thawed frozen whipped topping or whipped cream along with a piece of cake. Go for it—especially if the Bundt cake is simply dusted with confectioners' sugar or has a light glaze.

To whip heavy cream, pour it into a deep bowl. It will whip faster if the bowl and beaters are cold. To keep splatters to a minimum, begin beating on low speed with a handheld mixer, then gradually increase the speed to medium-high. Gradually beat in about 2 tablespoons confectioners' sugar

per cup of cream, or sweeten to taste, and continue beating until the cream holds stiff peaks. ("Stiff peaks" means the cream will hold its shape when you lift the beaters out of the bowl.)

Equipment to Use for Bundt Cakes

Wire rack: Most of the recipes recommend setting the cake on a wire rack to cool.

Mixer: Many of the recipes recommend using an electric mixer and most of the recipes work well with a handheld mixer. If a larger, heavy-duty stand mixer is needed, it will state so in the recipe.

Whisk: We often recommend whisking the flour with the leavening ingredients and salt so they are thoroughly blended and aerated before adding them to the liquids.

BUNDT CAKE BLISS

Southern Praline Bundt Cake . . . 17

Italian Cream Bundt Cake . . . 18

Kentucky Bourbon Bundt Cake . . . 20

Apple Cider Bundt Cake . . . 20

Crème Fraîche Bundt Cake . . . 21

Sour Cream Bundt Cake . . . 21

Watergate Bundt Cake . . . 22

Birthday Bundt Cake . . . 25

Chocolate Birthday Bundt Cake . . . 25

Rosemary-Lemon Bundt Cake . . . 26

Orange Date Nut Bundt Cake . . . 28

Brown Sugar Date Nut Bundt Cake . . . 28

French Apple Bundt Cake . . . 30

Almond-Olive Oil Bundt Cake . . . 32

Apricot Almond Bundt Cake . . . 32

Strawberry Bundt Cake with Balsamic Strawberry Sauce . . . 34

Sweet Tea Bundt Cake . . . 36

Orange Sweet Tea Bundt Cake . . . 36

Pineapple-Coconut Bundt Cake . . . 37

Golden Pineapple Bundt Cake . . . 37

Almond–Poppy Seed Bundt Cake . . . 38

Lemon–Poppy Seed Bundt Cake . . . 38

Zucchini–Thyme Bundt Cake . . . 39

Cappuccino Bundt Cake . . . 40

Caramel Macchiato Bundt Cake . . . 40

Pineapple Upside-Down Bundt Cake . . . 41

Tomato Soup Spice Bundt Cake . . . 43

Southern Praline Bundt Cake

MAKES 1 BUNDT CAKE

When a trip to the French Market in New Orleans is just not possible, enjoy the next best thing. Savor a slice of this Southern Praline Bundt Cake and sip on chicory coffee. Better yet, invite friends over and create your own version of Southern hospitality. "Let the good times roll!"

Nonstick baking spray with flour

3 cups all-purpose flour

1 teaspoon baking powder

½ teaspoon salt

1 cup (2 sticks) unsalted butter, softened

½ cup solid vegetable shortening

3 cups packed brown sugar

2 teaspoons pure vanilla extract

5 large eggs

1 cup buttermilk

1 cup coarsely chopped pecans, toasted (see page 12)

Praline Icing (page 150)

1. Preheat the oven to 325°F. Spray a 15-cup Bundt pan with nonstick baking spray with flour.
2. In a medium bowl, whisk together the flour, baking powder, and salt; set aside.
3. In the bowl of a stand mixer fitted with the paddle attachment, beat together the butter, shortening, brown sugar, and vanilla on medium-high speed for 3 to 5 minutes, or until light and fluffy. Beat in the eggs one at a time, beating well after each addition.
4. With the mixer on low speed, beat in the flour mixture in three additions, alternating with the buttermilk, beginning and ending with the flour. Stir in the pecans by hand.
5. Spoon the batter into the prepared pan. Bake for 50 to 60 minutes, or until a wooden pick inserted into the center comes out clean.
6. Place the cake on a wire rack to cool for 10 minutes. Invert the cake onto the rack and let cool completely.
7. Set the cake on the rack over a sheet of parchment paper to catch any drips and drizzle with the Praline Icing.

TIPS:

For a decorative presentation, place pecan halves evenly over the top of the iced cake.

Bundt cakes make delicious cupcake-size Bundt cakes (often called Bundtlettes) or small cakes. Spray the pan with nonstick baking spray with flour, then fill the pan about one-half to two-thirds full of batter. Bake, using the oven temperature stated in the recipe, but reduce the baking time. Generally begin checking for doneness after about 15 minutes, then watch carefully to avoid overbaking. Bake the cake until a wooden pick inserted into the center comes out clean.

Italian Cream Bundt Cake

MAKES 1 BUNDT CAKE

There isn't much authentic history regarding the origin of Italian cream cake, but it appears to be more of a favorite in the Southern United States and not so much in Italy. It's definitely a favorite of folks who enjoy creamy and crunchy with every bite, even if they live north of the Mason-Dixon Line. This moist, flavorful Italian Cream Bundt Cake is perfect for any occasion but is especially well suited for family gatherings or potlucks, where lots of people can enjoy a slice—there will be plenty to go around.

Nonstick baking spray with flour
1 (15.25- to 18-ounce) box white or vanilla cake mix
4 large eggs
1¼ cups buttermilk
¼ cup vegetable or canola oil
1 teaspoon pure vanilla extract
1 cup sweetened flaked coconut
1 cup chopped pecans, toasted (see page 12), plus more for garnish
Cream Cheese Glaze (page 143)
Toasted coconut (see Tip), for garnish

TIP:

To toast coconut, preheat the oven to 350°F. Spread the coconut evenly over a rimmed baking sheet. Bake, stirring occasionally, for 7 to 8 minutes, or until the coconut is light golden brown. Let cool completely before sprinkling the coconut on the glazed cake.

1. Preheat the oven to 350°F. Spray a 10-cup Bundt pan with nonstick baking spray with flour.
2. In a large bowl using a handheld mixer on low speed, blend together the cake mix, eggs, buttermilk, oil, and vanilla. Scrape down the sides of the bowl well and beat on medium speed for 2 minutes. Fold in the coconut and pecans by hand.
3. Pour the batter into the prepared pan. Bake for 35 to 45 minutes, or until a wooden pick inserted into the center comes out clean.
4. Place the cake on a wire rack to cool for 10 minutes. Invert the cake onto the rack to cool completely.
5. Set the cake on the rack over a sheet of parchment paper to catch any drips and drizzle with the Cream Cheese Glaze. Sprinkle evenly with toasted pecans and toasted coconut.
6. Store the cake in the refrigerator until ready to serve. Keep any leftovers refrigerated.

Kentucky Bourbon Bundt Cake

MAKES 1 BUNDT CAKE

We recently spent some time in Louisville, Kentucky, at a culinary conference. That road trip convinced us that everything is better with bourbon!

Nonstick baking spray with flour
2¾ cups all-purpose flour
1 teaspoon baking powder
1 teaspoon baking soda
1 teaspoon salt
1 cup (2 sticks) unsalted butter, softened
1 cup granulated sugar
1 cup packed brown sugar
5 large eggs
3 tablespoons bourbon
1 cup buttermilk
Bourbon Glaze (page 145)

1. Preheat the oven to 350°F. Spray a 10- or 12-cup Bundt pan with nonstick baking spray with flour.
2. In a medium bowl, whisk together the flour, baking powder, baking soda, and salt; set aside.
3. In a large bowl, beat together the butter, granulated sugar, and brown sugar with a handheld mixer on medium-high speed for 3 to 5 minutes, or until light and fluffy. Add the eggs one at a time, beating well after each egg and scraping down the sides of the bowl as needed.
4. In a measuring cup, stir together the bourbon and buttermilk. With the mixer on low speed, beat in the flour mixture in three steps, alternating with the buttermilk mixture, beginning and ending with the flour.
5. Pour the batter into the prepared pan. Bake for 40 to 50 minutes, or until a wooden pick inserted into the center comes out clean.
6. Place the cake on a wire rack set over a sheet of parchment paper. While the cake is still in the pan, use a skewer to poke holes in the cake. Drizzle the cake with about two-thirds of the Bourbon Glaze. Invert the cake onto the rack. Brush the remaining glaze over the top of the cake. Allow the cake to cool completely.

VARIATION:

Apple Cider Bundt Cake
Substitute apple cider for the bourbon. Prepare and bake the cake as directed. Glaze with Apple Cider Glaze (page 145) instead of Bourbon Glaze.

TIP:

If desired, add ¾ cup chopped toasted pecans to the batter before baking (see page 12 for instructions on toasting nuts).

For a delicious and beautiful presentation, slice the cake and serve each slice with fresh berries on top, then dollop with whipped cream.

Crème Fraîche Bundt Cake

MAKES 1 BUNDT CAKE

It's no secret that Roxanne would move to France in a heartbeat if given the opportunity. In the meantime, she travels there whenever she can and incorporates the French way of cooking into her routine as much as she can. Crème fraîche is easy enough to make (see Tip).

Nonstick baking spray with flour

3 cups all-purpose flour

¼ teaspoon baking powder

½ teaspoon salt

1 cup (2 sticks) unsalted butter, softened

1 cup packed brown sugar

1 cup granulated sugar

6 large eggs

1 teaspoon pure vanilla extract

1 cup crème fraîche (see Tip)

Confectioners' sugar, for garnish (optional)

1. Preheat the oven to 325°F. Spray a 10-cup Bundt pan with nonstick baking spray with flour.
2. In a medium bowl, whisk together the flour, baking powder, and salt; set aside.
3. In a large bowl using a handheld mixer, beat together the butter, brown sugar, and granulated sugar on medium-high speed for 3 to 5 minutes, or until light and fluffy. Beat in the eggs one at a time, beating well after each addition and scraping the sides of the bowl as needed. Add the vanilla and blend well.
4. Stir half the flour mixture into the creamed mixture. (Do not use a mixer.) Add the crème fraîche and stir gently to combine. Add the remaining flour mixture and gently stir until well incorporated.
5. Spoon the batter into the prepared pan. Bake for 45 to 55 minutes, or until a wooden pick inserted into the center comes out clean.
6. Place the cake on a wire rack to cool for 10 minutes. Invert the cake onto the rack and let cool for 1 hour.
7. If desired, set the cake on the rack over a sheet of parchment paper and sift confectioners' sugar over the top to garnish.

VARIATION:

Sour Cream Bundt Cake
Substitute sour cream for the crème fraîche. Prepare and bake the cake as directed.

TIPS:

Crème fraîche is available at some grocery stores, but if you would like to make your own, it is easy. In a small bowl, stir together 1½ tablespoons buttermilk and 1 cup heavy cream. Allow the mixture to stand, covered, at room temperature for 8 hours. Stir, cover, and refrigerate until ready to use. Measure out 1 cup crème fraîche to use in this recipe.

For a delicious and beautiful presentation, slice cake and place it on a serving plate. Top with fresh fruit and a dollop of crème fraîche.

Watergate Bundt Cake

MAKES 1 BUNDT CAKE

This retro recipe takes us back to the days of the Watergate scandal. The title was given to the event that took place forty-five years ago when there was a break-in at the Democratic National Party headquarters in the Watergate Hotel in Washington, D.C. By 1976, Watergate cake was all the rage, and to this day many a potluck or Thanksgiving feast would not be complete without this iconic recipe.

Nonstick baking spray with flour
1 (3.4-ounce) box pistachio instant pudding mix
1 (15.25- to 18-ounce) box white cake mix
3 large eggs
1 cup vegetable or canola oil
1 cup club soda or sparkling water
½ cup chopped pecans, toasted (see page 12)
1 cup confectioners' sugar
2 tablespoons whole milk
Chopped pistachios or pecans, for garnish (optional)

TIPS:

If desired, add 1 or 2 drops green food coloring to the glaze. You can substitute still water for the club soda or sparkling water.

1. Preheat the oven to 325°F. Spray a 10-cup Bundt pan with nonstick baking spray with flour.
2. Set aside 2 tablespoons of the instant pudding mix for use in the glaze.
3. In a large bowl using a handheld mixer, blend together the cake mix, remaining pudding mix, eggs, oil, and club soda on low speed. Scrape down the sides of the bowl well and beat for 2 minutes on medium speed. Stir in the chopped pecans.
4. Pour the batter into the prepared pan. Bake for 40 to 50 minutes, or until a wooden pick inserted into the center comes out clean.
5. Place the cake on a wire rack to cool for 10 minutes. Invert the cake onto the rack and let cool completely.
6. Meanwhile, in a small bowl, whisk together the reserved 2 tablespoons pudding mix, the confectioners' sugar, and the milk until smooth.
7. Set the cake on the rack over a sheet of parchment paper to catch any drips. Pour the glaze evenly over the cake. Sprinkle with chopped pistachios or pecans, if desired.

Birthday Bundt Cake

MAKES 1 BUNDT CAKE

Don't you dare visit the trendy bakery down the street or go to the grocery store bakery and "pick up" a birthday cake when you have the secret to a perfect birthday celebration right under your nose. The convenience of cake mix makes this Birthday Bundt Cake a go-to celebration cake, and no one can resist smiling when they see the sprinkles both inside and out!

Nonstick baking spray with flour
1 (15.25- to 18-ounce) box vanilla or white cake mix
1 (3.4-ounce) box vanilla instant pudding mix
1¼ cups whole milk
½ cup vegetable or canola oil
3 large eggs
1½ teaspoons pure vanilla extract
½ cup sprinkles, plus more for garnish
White Chocolate Glaze (page 148)

1. Preheat the oven to 350°F. Spray a 10-cup Bundt pan with nonstick baking spray with flour.
2. In a large bowl using a handheld mixer, blend together the cake mix, pudding mix, milk, oil, eggs, and vanilla on low speed. Scrape down the sides of the bowl well and beat on medium speed for 2 minutes. Fold in the sprinkles by hand.
3. Pour the batter into the prepared pan. Bake for 40 to 50 minutes, or until a wooden pick inserted into the center comes out clean.
4. Place the cake on a wire rack to cool for 10 minutes. Invert the cake onto the rack and let cool completely.
5. Set the cake on the rack over a sheet of parchment paper to catch any drips and drizzle with the White Chocolate Glaze. Garnish with additional sprinkles.

VARIATION:

Chocolate Birthday Bundt Cake
Substitute chocolate cake mix for the vanilla cake mix and chocolate instant pudding mix for the vanilla instant pudding mix. Prepare and bake the cake as directed. Drizzle with the White Chocolate Glaze as directed, then garnish with sprinkles.

TIP:

You could substitute a box of yellow cake mix for the white cake mix.

Rosemary-Lemon Bundt Cake

MAKES 1 BUNDT CAKE

Sweet and tender with the perfect tint of yellow flecked with rosemary makes this Rosemary-Lemon Bundt Cake intriguing. Roxanne once offered a slice to her neighbor, who exclaimed, "Oh, no, thank you, I love lemon, but rosemary, not so much." Roxanne insisted she give this one a try, and guess what? The flavor combo was a winner, and Roxanne sent plenty of cake home for her neighbor to enjoy. This is a winner—give it a try!

Nonstick baking spray with flour
3 cups all-purpose flour
2 teaspoons baking powder
½ teaspoon salt
1 cup (2 sticks) unsalted butter, softened
1¾ cups granulated sugar
4 large eggs
1½ teaspoons lemon extract
1 teaspoon pure vanilla extract
1 cup buttermilk
1 tablespoon grated lemon zest, plus more for garnish, if desired
3 tablespoons finely chopped fresh rosemary, plus a sprig or two for garnish, if desired
Lemon Glaze (page 144)

TIP:

We prefer the flavor of this cake with the lemon zest, but in a pinch you could omit it.

1. Preheat the oven to 350°F. Spray a 10-cup Bundt pan with nonstick baking spray with flour.
2. In a medium bowl, whisk together the flour, baking powder, and salt; set aside.
3. In a large bowl using a handheld mixer, beat together the butter and sugar on medium-high speed for 3 to 5 minutes, or until light and fluffy. Beat in the eggs one at a time, beating well after each addition. Add the lemon extract and the vanilla and beat well.
4. With the mixer on low speed, beat in the flour mixture in three additions, alternating with the buttermilk, beginning and ending with the flour. Stir the lemon zest and rosemary into the batter by hand.
5. Spoon the batter into the prepared pan. Bake for 40 to 50 minutes, or until a wooden pick inserted into the center comes out clean.

6. Place the cake on a wire rack to cool for 10 minutes. Invert the cake onto the rack and let cool for another 10 minutes.

7. Set the cake on the rack over a sheet of parchment paper to catch any drips. Use a skewer to poke holes in the cake and drizzle the Lemon Glaze over the cake. If desired, sprinkle with lemon zest and stick a sprig or two of rosemary into the cake to garnish.

Orange Date Nut Bundt Cake

MAKES 1 BUNDT CAKE

This recipe for Orange Date Nut Bundt Cake is versatile, and the cake can be made ahead a day or two in advance, wrapped tightly, and still be delicious to serve. You can call it a cake, but we often serve this at brunch as a coffee cake when we are entertaining guests. Either way, it is scrumptious!

Nonstick baking spray with flour
3½ cups all-purpose flour
1¼ teaspoons baking soda
1 cup (2 sticks) unsalted butter, softened
1¾ cups granulated sugar
4 large eggs
1 teaspoon pure vanilla extract
1½ cups buttermilk
1 cup chopped pitted dates
1 cup chopped pecans, toasted (see page 12)
1 tablespoon grated orange zest
Orange Glaze (page 145)

VARIATION:

Brown Sugar Date Nut Bundt Cake Omit the orange zest. Substitute 1 cup granulated sugar and ¾ cup brown sugar for the 1¾ cups granulated sugar. Prepare and bake the cake as directed. Glaze with the Brown Sugar Glaze (page 151) instead of Orange Glaze.

1. Preheat the oven to 350°F. Spray a 10-cup Bundt pan with nonstick baking spray with flour.
2. Set aside 1 tablespoon of the flour.
3. In a medium bowl, whisk together the remaining flour and the baking soda; set aside.
4. In a large bowl using a handheld mixer, beat together the butter and sugar on medium-high speed for 3 to 5 minutes, or until light and fluffy. Beat in the eggs one at a time, beating well after each addition. Add the vanilla and beat well.
5. With the mixer on low speed, beat in the flour mixture in three additions, alternating with the buttermilk, beginning and ending with the flour.
6. Toss the dates with the reserved 1 tablespoon flour. Stir the dates, pecans, and orange zest into the batter by hand.

TIP:

Toasting the pecans intensifies their flavor (see page 12 for instructions on toasting nuts).

7. Pour the batter into the prepared pan. Bake for 50 to 60 minutes, or until a wooden pick inserted into the center comes out clean.

8. Place the cake on a wire rack to cool for 10 minutes. While the cake is still in the pan, use a skewer to poke holes in the cake. Pour half the Orange Glaze over the cake, then immediately invert the cake onto a serving platter. Poke the top of the cake with the skewer and pour the remaining Orange Glaze over the top. Allow the cake to cool.

French Apple Bundt Cake

MAKES 1 BUNDT CAKE

Do you question if the words "French" and "easy" go together in the same sentence? This time, they really do. Classic French yogurt cake, which is the basis for this French Apple Bundt Cake, is a very simple cake. Just grab a whisk and you will be done in a moment. The delicious cake is like a dessert palette, just waiting for a glaze or fruit topping. This time, we took that timeless yogurt cake, added apple for a flavor twist, and glazed it with a brandy glaze. The result is a delightful apple cake that can be served any time of year.

Nonstick baking spray with flour

2 cups plus 1 tablespoon all-purpose flour

1½ teaspoons baking powder

½ teaspoon baking soda

¼ teaspoon salt

1 medium Granny Smith apple, peeled, cored, and very finely chopped

1 cup plain whole-milk yogurt

¾ cup granulated sugar

⅓ cup vegetable or canola oil

2 large eggs

2 teaspoons pure vanilla extract

Apple Brandy Glaze

½ cup apple juice

¼ cup granulated sugar

3 tablespoons apple brandy, applejack brandy, or brandy

TIPS:

The French are known for Calvados, a famous and excellently flavored apple brandy. If you don't have Calvados, you can use applejack brandy or brandy.

While low-fat yogurt is common, whole-milk yogurt is now readily available. In a pinch, you could substitute plain low-fat yogurt or sour cream for the whole-milk yogurt in this cake recipe.

1. Preheat the oven to 350°F. Spray a 10-cup Bundt pan with nonstick baking spray with flour.
2. In a medium bowl, whisk together 2 cups of the flour, the baking powder, baking soda, and salt; set aside.
3. In a small bowl, stir together the apple and the remaining 1 tablespoon flour; set aside.
4. In a large bowl, whisk together the yogurt, sugar, oil, eggs, and vanilla. Whisk in the flour mixture until moistened. Stir in the apple mixture.

5. Spoon the batter into the prepared pan. Bake for 35 to 45 minutes, or until a wooden pick inserted into the center comes out clean.

6. Place the cake on a wire rack to cool for 10 minutes. Invert the cake onto the rack and let cool completely.

7. Meanwhile, make the Apple Brandy Glaze: In a small saucepan, bring the apple juice to a boil over medium heat. Reduce the heat to maintain a simmer and cook, uncovered, for 5 to 6 minutes or until the juice has reduced by about half. (Watch carefully so the pan doesn't boil dry.) Stir in the sugar and cook, stirring continuously, until the sugar has dissolved. Remove from the heat. Stir in the brandy.

8. Set the cake on the rack over a sheet of parchment paper. Using a skewer, poke holes evenly over the top of the cake. Using a pastry brush, brush the glaze evenly over the cake, covering it completely. Drizzle the remaining glaze slowly over the top of the cake.

Almond–Olive Oil Bundt Cake

MAKES 1 BUNDT CAKE

We use olive oil for many cooking tasks, but using it in a cake may not be something you have thought about doing. Olive oil bakes into a delicious, moist cake with a slightly firm yet yummy texture. The chopped almonds in the cake add a delightful crunch, but the crowning glory is the Almond-Cream Glaze. That firmer texture makes this an ideal cake to pack up and take outside to the picnic, the tailgate, or any time you want a sweet treat that will travel to the party. And since Kathy is always ready to eat alfresco and is a true fan of almond flavors, this Almond–Olive Oil Bundt Cake is one she makes again and again.

Nonstick baking spray with flour
2¼ cups all-purpose flour
2½ teaspoons baking powder
½ teaspoon baking soda
½ teaspoon salt
1 cup olive oil
1½ cups granulated sugar
4 large eggs
¼ cup sour cream
¼ cup whole milk
1 teaspoon almond extract
½ cup sliced almonds, toasted (see page 12) and finely chopped

Almond-Cream Glaze

3 tablespoons unsalted butter
3 tablespoons granulated sugar
3 tablespoons heavy cream
¼ cup sliced almonds, toasted (see page 12)
¼ teaspoon almond extract

1. Preheat the oven to 350°F. Spray a 10-cup Bundt pan with nonstick baking spray with flour.
2. In a medium bowl, whisk together the flour, baking powder, baking soda, and salt; set aside.

VARIATION:

Apricot Almond Bundt Cake Prepare and bake the cake as directed. Cool the cake completely. Use a serrated knife and slice the Bundt cake in half horizontally.

In a small microwave-safe glass bowl, microwave ½ cup apricot preserves on High (100%) power for 30 seconds. Stir to make the preserves smooth. Place the bottom half of the cake on a serving platter and spread the preserves evenly on top. Top with the remaining half of the cake, cut side down. Glaze with the Almond-Cream Glaze as directed.

3. In a large bowl using a handheld mixer, beat together the olive oil and sugar on medium-high speed for 1 minute. Beat in the eggs one at a time, beating well after each addition. Beat in the sour cream, milk, and almond extract.

4. With the mixer on low speed, blend in the flour mixture. Stir in the chopped almonds.

5. Pour the batter into the prepared pan. Bake for 40 to 50 minutes or until wooden pick inserted into the center comes out clean.

6. Place the cake on a wire rack to cool for 10 minutes. Invert the cake onto the rack and let cool completely.

7. Meanwhile, make the Almond-Cream Glaze: In a small saucepan, melt the butter over low heat. Stir in the sugar and cook, stirring, for 1 minute, or until the sugar has dissolved. Stir in the cream and cook, stirring, for 1 minute. Stir in the almonds. Remove from the heat and stir in the almond extract.

8. Set the cake on the rack over a sheet of parchment paper to catch any drips and drizzle the Almond-Cream Glaze over the cake.

Strawberry Bundt Cake with Balsamic Strawberry Sauce

MAKES 1 BUNDT CAKE

Strawberry picking is a cherished tradition for us. We wait for the farmer to announce the opening day. Fresh-picked strawberries are the best berries, and they drip with juice, so anything you make using them tastes superb. But when you love strawberries like we do, you crave that flavor all year long, and this Strawberry Bundt Cake with Balsamic Strawberry Sauce delivers! It really is delicious, even if the berries you are using don't come from a local farm. The drizzle of balsamic vinegar in the strawberry sauce adds a great distinctive flavor.

Nonstick baking spray with flour

¼ cup finely chopped fresh strawberries

1 tablespoon water

1 (15.25- to 18-ounce) box white cake mix

2 (6-ounce) cartons low-fat strawberry yogurt

3 large egg whites

⅓ cup vegetable or canola oil

4 or 5 drops red food coloring (optional)

TIP:

If desired, drizzle the cake with Vanilla Glaze (page 142) instead of dusting with confectioners' sugar.

Balsamic Strawberry Sauce

2 tablespoons granulated sugar

2 teaspoons cornstarch

2 tablespoons water

2 cups chopped fresh strawberries

1 tablespoon balsamic vinegar

Confectioners' sugar, for garnish

1. Preheat the oven to 325°F. Spray a 10-cup Bundt pan with nonstick baking spray with flour.
2. In a large bowl, combine the finely chopped strawberries and water. Mash the strawberries with the back of a spoon to release their juices. Let stand for 5 minutes.
3. Add the cake mix, yogurt, egg whites, oil, and food coloring to the mashed strawberry mixture and use a handheld mixer on low speed to

blend the mixture together. Scrape down the sides of the bowl well and beat for 2 minutes on medium speed.

4. Pour the batter into the prepared pan. Bake for 45 to 55 minutes, or until a wooden pick inserted into the center comes out clean.

5. Place the cake on a wire rack to cool for 10 minutes. Invert the cake onto the rack and let cool completely.

6. Meanwhile, make the Balsamic Strawberry Sauce: In a small saucepan, stir together the granulated sugar and cornstarch. Stir in the water and stir until the sugar and cornstarch have completely dissolved. Stir in the strawberries. Cook over low heat, stirring occasionally, for 10 to 11 minutes, or until the berries become very juicy, the mixture boils, and the liquids become clear. Remove from the heat and stir in the vinegar. Allow the sauce to cool.

7. Set the cake on the rack over a sheet of parchment paper. Sift confectioners' sugar over the top of the cake. Slice the cake and serve each slice with a spoonful of Balsamic Strawberry Sauce on top.

Sweet Tea Bundt Cake

MAKES 1 BUNDT CAKE

Front porches lined with comfy chairs and big, frosty glasses of sweet tea sitting on the table nearby. It sounds like a movie about life in the South, but it is reality. Sweet tea is the favorite drink in the South when friends visit and need a break from the summer heat. This Sweet Tea Bundt Cake relies on that iconic beverage to capture an inviting, not-too-sweet taste. Add the Lemon Glaze, and your guests will be asking for a second slice.

Nonstick baking spray with flour
2½ cups all-purpose flour
1⅓ cups granulated sugar
1½ teaspoons baking powder
1 teaspoon baking soda
½ teaspoon salt
Grated zest of 1 lemon
1 cup sour cream
3 large eggs
1 cup sweet tea
½ cup (1 stick) unsalted butter, melted
⅓ cup vegetable or canola oil
Lemon Glaze (page 144)

1. Preheat the oven to 350°F. Spray a 10-cup Bundt pan with nonstick baking spray with flour.
2. In a large bowl, whisk together the flour, sugar, baking powder, baking soda, salt, and lemon zest. Add the sour cream, eggs, tea, melted butter, and oil and use a handheld mixer on low speed to blend well. Scrape down the sides of the bowl well and beat for 1 minute on medium speed.
3. Pour the batter into the prepared pan. Bake for 40 to 50 minutes, or until a wooden pick inserted into the center comes out clean.
4. Place the cake on a wire rack to cool for 10 minutes. Invert the cake onto the rack and let cool completely.
5. Set the cake on the rack over a sheet of parchment paper to catch any drips. Use a skewer to poke holes into the cake. Drizzle the Lemon Glaze over the cake.

VARIATION:

Orange Sweet Tea Bundt Cake

Substitute grated orange zest for the lemon zest. Prepare and bake the cake as directed. Glaze with Quick Orange Glaze (page 144) instead of Lemon Glaze.

TIP:

Sweet tea is available ready to use. If you prefer to make your own, place 1 tea bag in ¾ cup boiling water and steep for 15 minutes. To make the simple syrup traditionally used to sweeten the tea, stir together ¼ cup boiling water and ¼ cup sugar until the sugar has dissolved. Remove and discard the tea bag. Pour the simple syrup into the tea to make 1 cup sweet tea.

Pineapple-Coconut Bundt Cake

MAKES 1 BUNDT CAKE

A sweet treat is just the thing to share when celebrating the good times in life with a friend. This Pineapple–Coconut Bundt Cake, with its sunny yellow color and delightful pineapple and coconut flavor, is the ideal cake to serve at those happy times. It takes just minutes to whip up, since it begins with a mix, and it stays moist, so you can make it the day before serving.

Nonstick baking spray with flour
1 cup sweetened flaked coconut
1 cup whole milk
1 (15.25- to 18-ounce) box yellow cake mix
1 (3.4-ounce) box coconut cream instant pudding mix
4 large eggs
½ cup vegetable or canola oil
1 (20-ounce) can crushed pineapple in juice, well drained
Vanilla Glaze (page 142)
Sweetened flaked coconut, toasted (see page 18), for garnish

1. Preheat the oven to 325°F. Spray a 15-cup Bundt pan with nonstick baking spray with flour.
2. In a large bowl, stir together the coconut and milk. Allow to stand for 5 minutes.
3. Add the cake mix, pudding mix, eggs, and oil to the coconut-milk mixture and use a handheld mixer on low speed to blend well. Scrape down the sides of the bowl well and beat on medium speed for 2 minutes.
4. Stir the crushed pineapple into the cake batter by hand.
5. Spoon the batter into the prepared pan. Bake for 50 to 60 minutes, or until a wooden pick inserted into the center comes out clean.
6. Place the cake on a wire rack to cool for 10 minutes. Invert the cake onto the rack and let cool completely.
7. Set the cake on the rack over a sheet of parchment paper to catch any drips and drizzle with the Vanilla Glaze. Garnish with toasted coconut, if desired.

VARIATION:

Golden Pineapple Bundt Cake
Omit the sweetened, flaked coconut in the cake and as a garnish. Substitute vanilla or French vanilla instant pudding mix for the coconut cream instant pudding mix. Prepare and bake the cake as directed. Reserve the pineapple juice for use in the Pineapple Glaze. Glaze with the Pineapple Glaze (page 142) instead of Vanilla Glaze.

TIPS:

To drain the pineapple, place it in a strainer over a small bowl. Press the pineapple with the back of a spoon to drain well. The juice is not used in this cake, so discard it, enjoy it as a beverage, or use it in a smoothie or fruit salad.

Almond–Poppy Seed Bundt Cake

MAKES 1 BUNDT CAKE

Sometimes a slice of cake is just the perfect sweet treat to go with a cup of coffee or tea. You know the kind of cake we mean: a simple, great-tasting cake that is moist and, well, just perfect. This Almond–Poppy Seed Bundt Cake is that kind of cake.

Nonstick baking spray with flour
1 cup vanilla-flavored almond milk
2 tablespoons poppy seeds
1 (15.25- to 18-ounce) box yellow cake mix
4 large eggs
½ cup (1 stick) unsalted butter, melted
½ teaspoon almond extract
Vanilla Glaze (page 142) or Almond Glaze (page 142)

1. Preheat the oven to 350°F. Spray a 10-cup Bundt pan with the nonstick baking spray with flour.
2. In a large bowl, stir together the almond milk and poppy seeds. Allow the seeds to soak for 5 minutes.
3. Add the cake mix, eggs, melted butter, and almond extract to the almond milk mixture and use a handheld mixer on low speed to blend well. Scrape down the sides of the bowl well and beat on medium speed for 2 minutes.
4. Pour the batter into the prepared pan. Bake for 40 to 50 minutes, or until a wooden pick inserted into the center comes out clean.
5. Place the cake on a wire rack to cool for 10 minutes. Invert the cake onto the rack and let cool completely.
6. Set the cake on the rack over a sheet of parchment paper to catch any drips and drizzle with the Vanilla Glaze or Almond Glaze.

VARIATION:

Lemon Poppy Seed Bundt Cake
Substitute whole milk for the almond milk and lemon extract for the almond extract. Prepare and bake the cake as directed. Glaze with the Lemon Glaze (page 144) instead of the Vanilla or Almond Glaze.

TIP:

We love the delightful flavor the vanilla almond milk adds to this cake, but in a pinch, you could substitute whole milk.

Zucchini-Thyme Bundt Cake

MAKES 1 BUNDT CAKE

It seems that zucchini is either a blessing or a curse. Here in the Midwest, the vines are more than prolific from mid- to late summer, and zucchini show up in every possible dish! Lots of meals feature zucchini—maybe as a grilled vegetable dish, a cheesy casserole, spiraled zucchini noodles, or the ever-popular zucchini bread. But for a real treat, use it to make this Zucchini-Thyme Bundt Cake! The zucchini keeps the cake moist, and the thyme and lemon add fresh flavor.

Nonstick baking spray with flour
1 (15.25- to 18-ounce) box yellow cake mix
1 (3.4-ounce) box vanilla instant pudding mix
4 large eggs
¾ cup vegetable or canola oil
Grated zest of 1 lemon
3 tablespoons fresh lemon juice
1 teaspoon pure vanilla extract
2 cups shredded zucchini (about 1 medium zucchini), drained
1 tablespoon minced fresh thyme leaves
Lemon Glaze (page 144)

TIP:

To shred or grate the zucchini, trim off the stem end of the zucchini, then use a box grater (or the shredding disc on a food processor) to grate it. No need to peel the zucchini. Once grated, drain the zucchini if moisture collects, measure out 2 cups, and use it in this scrumptious cake.

1. Preheat the oven to 350°F. Spray a 12-cup Bundt pan with nonstick baking spray with flour.
2. In a large bowl using a handheld mixer, blend together the cake mix, pudding mix, eggs, oil, lemon zest, lemon juice, and vanilla on low speed. Scrape down the sides of the bowl well and beat on medium speed for 2 minutes. (The batter will be very thick.) Stir in the zucchini and thyme by hand.
3. Spoon the batter into the prepared pan. Bake for 40 to 50 minutes, or until a wooden pick inserted into the center comes out clean.
4. Place the cake on a wire rack to cool for 10 minutes. Invert the cake onto the rack and let cool completely.
5. Set the cake on the rack over a sheet of parchment paper to catch any drips. Use a skewer to poke holes into the cake. Drizzle the Lemon Glaze over the cake.

Cappuccino Bundt Cake

MAKES 1 BUNDT CAKE

Are you a cappuccino fan? Are you the one who stops at a coffee shop every morning and knows the name of your favorite barista? If so, this Cappuccino Bundt Cake is the one for you. It is such a treat because it combines all the flavors that you expect in your favorite cappucino—coffee, vanilla, cinnamon, and chocolate—in every delicious bite.

Nonstick baking spray with flour

1 cup mini semisweet chocolate chips

1 (15.25- to 18-ounce) box yellow cake mix

1 (3.4-ounce) box vanilla instant pudding mix

¼ cup instant espresso powder

1½ teaspoons ground cinnamon

4 large eggs

1 cup whole milk

½ cup vegetable or canola oil

2 teaspoons pure vanilla extract

Chocolate Glaze (page 146)

VARIATION:

Caramel Macchiato Bundt Cake
Omit the chocolate chips and cinnamon. Prepare and bake the cake as directed. Frost with the Caramel Icing (page 150) instead of the Chocolate Glaze.

TIP:

If desired, omit the chocolate chips. Prepare the batter as directed, using the entire box of cake mix. Bake as directed.

1. Preheat the oven to 350°F. Spray a 12-cup Bundt pan with nonstick baking spray with flour.
2. In a small bowl, toss together the mini chocolate chips and 1 table-spoon of the cake mix; set aside.
3. In a large bowl using a handheld mixer, blend together the remaining cake mix, the pudding mix, espresso powder, cinnamon, eggs, milk, oil, and vanilla on low speed. Scrape down the sides of the bowl well and beat on medium speed for 2 minutes. Stir in the chocolate chip mixture.
4. Pour the batter into the prepared pan. Bake for 40 to 50 minutes, or until a wooden pick inserted into the center comes out clean.
5. Place the cake on a wire rack to cool for 10 minutes. Invert the cake onto the rack and let cool completely.
6. Set the cake on the rack over a sheet of parchment paper to catch any drips and drizzle with the Chocolate Glaze.

Pineapple Upside-Down Bundt Cake

MAKES 1 BUNDT CAKE

This could easily become your showstopper cake recipe. The presentation is stunning, and the cake is equally impressive in taste and texture. The added maraschino cherries gild the lily. We like to serve this cake warm and enjoy the oohs and ahhs!

Nonstick baking spray with flour

1 (20-ounce) can pineapple slices in juice, drained, reserving juice

½ cup (1 stick) unsalted butter, cut into cubes

1 cup packed brown sugar

7 maraschino cherries, drained well

1 (15.25- to 18-ounce) box yellow cake mix

½ cup vegetable or canola oil

4 large eggs

1 teaspoon pure vanilla extract

TIP:

Enjoy the leftover pineapple slices for breakfast, lunch, or dinner!

1. Preheat the oven to 350°F. Spray a 10-cup Bundt pan with nonstick baking spray with flour.

2. In a small saucepan, combine 2 tablespoons of the reserved juice, butter, and brown sugar. Bring to a boil over medium heat; reduce the heat to low and simmer for 1 minute. Remove from the heat. Pour the brown sugar mixture into the prepared pan.

3. Arrange the drained pineapple slices in a single layer on top of the brown sugar mixture. (Depending on the size of your pan, you should be able to layer six or seven slices in the pan.) Place a maraschino cherry in the center of each pineapple slice.

4. Measure ¾ cup of the reserved pineapple juice (if needed, add water to equal ¾ cup). In a large bowl using a handheld mixer, blend together the cake mix, ¾ cup pineapple juice, oil, eggs, and vanilla on low speed. Scrape down the sides of the bowl well and beat on medium speed for 2 minutes.

5. Pour the batter into the pan over the pineapple slices. Bake for 35 to 45 minutes, or until a wooden pick inserted into the center comes out clean.

6. Using hot pads, immediately invert the cake onto a serving platter that has slight sides. Serve warm or at room temperature.

Tomato Soup Spice Bundt Cake

MAKES 1 BUNDT CAKE

Ewhhh! Don't even go down that rabbit hole. Do not judge this Tomato Soup Spice Bundt Cake until you try it. The smooth, rich spice flavor and ruby color studded with raisins are divine. Campbell's Soup claims this recipe first appeared in cookbooks in the early 1900s, but it wasn't until 1960 that the tomato soup cake recipe appeared on their label. Still as popular today as it ever was, we think you will give this version two thumbs up.

Nonstick baking spray with flour
1 (15.25- to 18-ounce) box spice cake mix
1 (10.75-ounce) can condensed tomato soup, undiluted
4 large eggs
$\frac{1}{3}$ cup vegetable or canola oil
$\frac{1}{2}$ cup buttermilk
$\frac{1}{2}$ cup raisins
Cream Cheese Glaze (page 143)

TIP:

If desired, stir ½ cup chopped toasted pecans into the batter when the raisins are added (see page 12 for instructions on toasting nuts). Or you can sprinkle the Cream Cheese Glaze with toasted pecans.

1. Preheat the oven to 350°F. Spray a 10-cup Bundt pan with nonstick baking spray with flour.
2. In a large bowl using a handheld mixer, blend together the cake mix, tomato soup, eggs, oil, and buttermilk on low speed. Scrape down the sides of the bowl well and beat on medium speed for 2 minutes. Stir in the raisins by hand.
3. Pour the batter into the prepared pan. Bake for 40 to 50 minutes, or until a wooden pick inserted into the center comes out clean.
4. Place the cake on a wire rack to cool for 10 minutes. Invert the cake onto the rack and let cool completely.
5. Set the cake on the rack over a sheet of parchment paper to catch any drips and drizzle with the Cream Cheese Glaze.
6. Store the cake in the refrigerator until ready to serve. Keep any leftovers refrigerated.

CHOCOLATE BUNDT CAKES

German Chocolate Bundt Cake

MAKES 1 BUNDT CAKE

Roxanne and her husband, Bob Bateman, rank German chocolate cake at the top of their list of favorites. But Roxanne seldom makes the traditional three-layer cake, as it takes a lot of time. This German Chocolate Bundt Cake has become her go-to recipe, and now she and Bob can enjoy the flavor of German chocolate cake without all the time and fuss. Bake the cake in one layer, and while the cake is baking, prepare the topping. Start to finish, this can be made in a little less than an hour.

Nonstick baking spray with flour
1 (15.25- to 18-ounce) box German chocolate cake mix
1 (3.9-ounce) box chocolate instant pudding mix
½ cup vegetable or canola oil
½ cup water
4 large eggs
1 cup sour cream
1 teaspoon pure vanilla extract

Coconut-Pecan Frosting

1 (6-ounce) can evaporated milk (note: this is the smaller can)
3 large egg yolks
1 teaspoon pure vanilla extract
¾ cup sugar
6 tablespoons (¾ stick) unsalted butter, cut into cubes
1½ cups sweetened flaked coconut
1 cup chopped pecans, toasted (see page 12)
Chocolate Glaze (page 146)

1. Preheat the oven to 350°F. Spray a 10-cup Bundt pan with nonstick baking spray with flour.
2. In a large bowl using a handheld mixer, blend together the cake mix, pudding mix, oil, water, eggs, sour cream, and vanilla on low speed. Scrape down the sides of the bowl well and beat on medium speed for 2 minutes.
3. Pour the batter into the prepared pan. Bake for 40 to 50 minutes, or until a wooden pick inserted into the center comes out clean.

4. Place the cake on a wire rack to cool for 10 minutes. Invert the cake onto the rack and let cool completely.

5. Meanwhile, make the Coconut-Pecan Frosting: In a medium saucepan, whisk together the evaporated milk, egg yolks, and vanilla. Stir in the sugar and butter. Cook over medium heat, stirring frequently, for 10 to 12 minutes, until the mixture thickens and turns a golden color. Remove from the heat and stir in the coconut and pecans. Pour into a bowl and refrigerate for at least 1 hour or until well chilled and thickened to the desired spreading consistency.

6. Set the cake on the rack over a sheet of parchment paper. Using a flat spreading spatula, frost the top of the Bundt cake with the Coconut-Pecan Frosting. Drizzle the Chocolate Glaze over the Coconut-Pecan Frosting.

7. Store the cake in the refrigerator until ready to serve. Keep any leftovers refrigerated.

Fudge Brownie Bundt Cake

MAKES 1 BUNDT CAKE

This recipe takes brownies to a new level, and it is a Father's Day treat for Roxanne's husband, Bob Bateman. He likes a slice of Fudge Brownie Cake topped with vanilla ice cream and drizzled with chocolate syrup. What dad wouldn't want to celebrate in similar fashion? Don't wait for a holiday to bake this brownie—make every day a celebration!

Nonstick baking spray with flour
1 (15.25- to 18-ounce) box devil's food or chocolate cake mix
1 (18.3-ounce) box (9 x 13-inch size) chewy fudge brownie mix
4 large eggs
1½ cups water
1 cup vegetable or canola oil
Chocolate Glaze (page 146)

TIP:

If desired, sprinkle ½ cup chopped toasted pecans on top of the glazed cake (see page 12 for instructions on toasting nuts).

1. Preheat the oven to 350°F. Spray a 15-cup Bundt pan with nonstick baking spray with flour.
2. In a large bowl using a handheld mixer, blend together the cake mix, brownie mix, eggs, water, and oil on low speed. Scrape down the sides of the bowl well and beat on medium speed until well combined, about 1 minute. Do not overbeat.
3. Spoon the batter into the prepared pan. Bake for 40 to 50 minutes, or until a wooden pick inserted into the center comes out clean.
4. Place the cake on a wire rack to cool for 10 minutes. Invert the cake onto the rack and let cool completely.
5. Set the cake on the rack over a sheet of parchment paper to catch any drips and drizzle with the Chocolate Glaze.

Turtle Bundt Cake

MAKES 1 BUNDT CAKE

Who can resist a decadent turtle candy? The same is true for this rich, ooey-gooey Turtle Bundt Cake. We feel certain it would win a blue ribbon at any state fair. The caramel icing is the secret to success in this recipe.

Nonstick baking spray with flour
1 (15.25- to 18-ounce) box devil's food cake mix
2 tablespoons unsweetened cocoa powder
1⅓ cups buttermilk
½ cup vegetable or canola oil
4 large eggs
1 teaspoon pure vanilla extract
Caramel Icing (page 150)
Chocolate Glaze (page 146)
⅓ cup chopped pecans, toasted (see page 12)

1. Preheat the oven to 350°F. Spray a 10-cup Bundt pan with nonstick baking spray with flour.

2. In a large bowl using a handheld mixer, blend together the cake mix, cocoa powder, buttermilk, oil, eggs, and vanilla on low speed. Scrape down the sides of the bowl well and beat on medium speed for 2 minutes.

3. Pour the batter into the prepared pan. Bake for 40 to 50 minutes, or until a wooden pick inserted into the center comes out clean.

4. Place the cake on a wire rack to cool for 10 minutes. Invert the cake onto the rack and let cool completely.

5. Set the cake on the rack over a sheet of parchment paper to catch any drips. Pour the Caramel Icing over the cake. Drizzle the Chocolate Glaze over the caramel. Sprinkle evenly with the pecans.

Triple Chocolate Bundt Cake

MAKES 1 BUNDT CAKE

Are you just a tad bit jealous of your friends who boast that they have a special birthday cake that they always prepare for their loved ones? Well, nothing more to be jealous over. This Triple Chocolate Bundt Cake is definitely a go-to celebration cake. Serve each slice with a scoop of your favorite ice cream, and you'll have your own tradition.

Nonstick baking spray with flour
1 (15.25- to 18-ounce) box devil's food cake mix
1 (5.9-ounce) box chocolate instant pudding mix (note: this is the larger box)
1¼ cups buttermilk
½ cup vegetable or canola oil
5 large eggs
1 teaspoon instant espresso powder
1 cup semisweet chocolate chips
Chocolate Glaze (page 146)

1. Preheat the oven to 350°F. Spray a 10-cup Bundt pan with nonstick baking spray with flour.
2. In a large bowl using a handheld mixer, blend together the cake mix, pudding mix, buttermilk, oil, eggs, and espresso powder on low speed. Scrape down the sides of the bowl well and beat on medium speed for 2 minutes. Stir in the chocolate chips by hand.
3. Pour the batter into the prepared pan. Bake for 40 to 50 minutes, or until a wooden pick inserted into the center comes out clean.
4. Place the cake on a wire rack to cool for 10 minutes. Invert the cake onto the rack and let cool completely.
5. Set the cake on the rack over a sheet of parchment paper to catch any drips and drizzle with the Chocolate Glaze.

TIPS:

One (12-ounce) package of semisweet chocolate chips is perfectly sized for making the cake and the glaze.

For an elegant garnish, drizzle the cake with the Chocolate Glaze as directed. Prepare the White Chocolate Glaze (page 148) and drizzle it back and forth over the chocolate glaze. The white and black appearance is stunning.

Espresso powder deepens the chocolate flavor. If you don't keep espresso powder on hand, you can omit it from the recipe.

VARIATIONS:

Chocolate Raspberry Bundt Cake

Omit the chocolate chips. Prepare and bake the cake as directed. Cool the cake completely. Use a serrated knife to slice the Bundt cake in half horizontally.

In a small, microwave-safe glass bowl, microwave ½ cup seedless raspberry preserves on High (100%) power for 30 seconds. Stir to make the preserves smooth. Place the bottom half of the cake on a serving platter and spread the preserves evenly on top. Top with the remaining half of the cake, cut side down. Glaze with Chocolate Glaze as directed and garnish with fresh raspberries.

Mint-Glazed Chocolate Bundt Cake

MAKES 1 BUNDT CAKE

What is the difference between mint and peppermint? "Mint" is an umbrella term used for the more than thirty varieties of mint that exist. Peppermint is one of the stronger mints and contains a higher amount of menthol. When purchasing extract, mint extract is a mixture of peppermint and spearmint, while peppermint extract is solely peppermint. All mint is refreshing, and combined with chocolate, it is absolute perfection!

Nonstick baking spray with flour
1 (15.25- to 18-ounce) box devil's food cake mix
1 (3.9-ounce) box instant chocolate pudding mix
¾ cup vegetable or canola oil
½ cup whole milk
4 large eggs
1 cup sour cream
1 teaspoon pure vanilla extract
1 teaspoon peppermint extract
1 (4.67-ounce) box crème de menthe thins
Chocolate-Mint Glaze (page 147)

1. Preheat the oven to 350°F. Spray a 10-cup Bundt pan with nonstick baking spray with flour.
2. In a large bowl using a handheld mixer, blend together the cake mix, pudding mix, oil, milk, eggs, sour cream, vanilla, and peppermint extract on low speed. Scrape down the sides of the bowl well and beat on medium speed for 2 minutes.
3. Unwrap and coarsely chop 7 of the crème de menthe thins; set aside. Unwrap and coarsely chop the remaining crème de menthe thins and fold them into the cake batter.
4. Pour the batter into the prepared pan. Bake for 40 to 50 minutes, or until a wooden pick inserted into the center comes out clean.
5. Place the cake on a wire rack to cool for 10 minutes. Invert the cake onto the rack and let cool completely.
6. Set the cake on the rack over a sheet of parchment paper to catch any drips and drizzle with the Chocolate-Mint Glaze. Sprinkle the reserved chopped crème de menthe thins evenly over the top.

Chocolate–Salted Caramel Bundt Cake

MAKES 1 BUNDT CAKE

To our thinking, when you marry chocolate and caramel and then add a dash of sea salt, you get nothing short of pure decadence. That is so very true for this truly luscious Chocolate– Salted Caramel Bundt Cake.

Nonstick baking spray with flour

1 (15.25- to 18-ounce) box devil's food cake mix

1 (3.9-ounce) box chocolate instant pudding mix

4 large eggs

1 cup sour cream

½ cup (1 stick) unsalted butter, melted

¼ cup whole milk

2 teaspoons pure vanilla extract

¾ cup caramel ice cream topping

½ teaspoon flaky sea salt, plus more for garnish

Chocolate Glaze (page 146)

TIP:

Ice cream topping or syrup? While similar, those labeled "ice cream topping" are thicker than syrup. For best results for this recipe, choose a thick ice cream topping. We prefer Mrs. Richardson's brand caramel topping.

1. Preheat the oven to 350°F. Spray a 12-cup Bundt pan with nonstick baking spray with flour.
2. In a large bowl using a handheld mixer, blend together the cake mix, pudding mix, eggs, sour cream, melted butter, milk, and vanilla on low speed. Scrape down the sides of the bowl well and beat on medium speed for 2 minutes. (The batter will be very thick.)
3. Spoon the batter into the prepared pan. Bake for 40 to 50 minutes, or until a wooden pick inserted into the center comes out clean.
4. Place the cake on a wire rack to cool for 10 minutes. Invert the cake onto the rack and set over a sheet of parchment paper to catch drips.
5. In a small microwave-safe glass bowl, microwave ¼ cup of the caramel ice cream topping on High (100%) power for 15 seconds, or until just warm. Stir the flaky sea salt into the warm caramel.
6. Using a skewer, poke holes over the top of the cake. Slowly drizzle the warm caramel over the cake, filling the holes. Allow the cake to cool completely.
7. Drizzle the cake with the Chocolate Glaze. Drizzle the remaining ½ cup caramel topping over the glaze. Sprinkle with salt to garnish.

White Chocolate Bundt Cake with Pomegranate Glaze

MAKES 1 BUNDT CAKE

White Chocolate Bundt Cake is rich and moist thanks to the white chocolate, and just the very mention of this cake evokes thoughts of celebrations and elegant dinners. White chocolate doesn't contain chocolate liqueur so it really isn't chocolate, but it is still sweet and delicious, and we predict you will be making this cake for lots of birthday parties and special events. For a crowning touch, add a beautiful light pink glaze quickly made from pomegranate juice.

Nonstick baking spray with flour

1 (4-ounce) bar white chocolate, chopped

2 cups all-purpose flour

½ teaspoon baking soda

¼ teaspoon salt

¾ cup (1½ sticks) unsalted butter, softened

1⅓ cups granulated sugar

3 large eggs

1 teaspoon pure vanilla extract

⅓ cup buttermilk

Pomegranate Glaze (page 148)

VARIATION:

White Chocolate Bundt Cake
Prepare and bake the cake as directed. Drizzle with White Chocolate Glaze (page 148) instead of the Pomegranate Glaze. Garnish the cake with fresh strawberries or raspberries.

1. Preheat the oven to 325°F. Spray a 10-cup Bundt pan with nonstick baking spray with flour.
2. In a small microwave-safe glass bowl, microwave the white chocolate on High (100%) power in 20-second intervals, stirring after each, until the white chocolate is melted and smooth. (Watch carefully to avoid scorching.) Set aside and allow to cool.
3. In a medium bowl, whisk together the flour, baking soda, and salt; set aside.
4. In a large bowl using a handheld mixer, beat together the butter and sugar on medium-high speed for 3 to 5 minutes, or until light and fluffy. Beat in the eggs one at a time, beating well after each addition. Beat in the vanilla and the melted white chocolate.

5. With the mixer on low speed, beat in the flour mixture in three additions, alternating with the buttermilk, beginning and ending with the flour.

6. Pour the batter into the prepared pan. Bake for 40 to 50 minutes, or until a wooden pick inserted into the center comes out clean.

7. Place the cake on a wire rack to cool for 10 minutes. Invert the cake onto the rack and let cool completely.

8. Set the cake on the rack over a sheet of parchment paper to catch any drips and drizzle with the Pomegranate Glaze.

Cookies 'n' Cream Bundt Cake

MAKES 1 BUNDT CAKE

Cookies 'n' Cream Bundt Cake is the ideal cake to donate to a bake sale, as it will sell quickly for a premium price. Or volunteer to take it to the office, because all your colleagues will clamor for a piece. Why is that? Well, everyone loves cream-filled chocolate cookies, and those wonderful cookies are stirred right into the cake. And since it is topped with more cookies, it is beautiful and looks extravagant. On top of that, it is quick to make from a mix. What more could you ask for?

Nonstick baking spray with flour
1 (15.25- to 18-ounce) box devil's food cake mix
1 (3.9-ounce) box chocolate instant pudding mix
4 large eggs
$\frac{1}{3}$ cup canola or vegetable oil
1 cup sour cream
$\frac{1}{2}$ cup whole milk
1 teaspoon pure vanilla extract
12 vanilla cream–filled chocolate sandwich cookies, coarsely
   crushed, plus 10 to 12 whole cookies for garnish
Rich Cream Glaze (page 143)

1. Preheat the oven to 350°F. Spray a 15-cup Bundt pan with nonstick baking spray with flour.
2. In a large bowl using a handheld mixer, blend together the cake mix, pudding mix, eggs, oil, sour cream, milk, and vanilla on low speed. Scrape down the sides of the bowl well and beat on medium speed for 2 minutes. Stir in the crushed cookies.
3. Spoon the batter into the prepared pan. Bake for 45 to 55 minutes, or until a wooden pick inserted into the center comes out clean.
4. Place the cake on a wire rack to cool for 10 minutes. Invert the cake onto the rack and let cool completely.
5. Set the cake on the rack over a sheet of parchment paper to catch any drips and drizzle with the Rich Cream Glaze.
6. Cut 5 or 6 of the cookies in half and arrange the halves upright, cut-side down, around the top of the cake. Finely crush the remaining 5 or 6 cookies and sprinkle the crumbs over the top of the cake.

Chocolate Tweed Bundt Cake

MAKES 1 BUNDT CAKE

"Tweed" refers to a distinctive, textured, woven fabric that is typically flaked with color, and you might associate that fabric with a sports coat or maybe a heavy woolen scarf. Seems an odd word to use to describe a cake, doesn't it? Well, think about a delicious white cake flaked with chocolate. The unique look of this baked cake will remind you of the fabric. The grated chocolate creates a flaked appearance, but the flavor is nothing short of luscious.

Nonstick baking spray with flour

2 (4-ounce) bars bittersweet chocolate

2 cups plus 1 tablespoon all-purpose flour

1 teaspoon baking powder

¼ teaspoon salt

¾ cup (1½ sticks) unsalted butter, softened

1⅓ cups granulated sugar

3 large eggs

1 teaspoon pure vanilla extract

⅓ cup whole milk

1 (4-ounce) bar white chocolate, chopped

1. Preheat the oven to 325°F. Spray a 12-cup Bundt pan with nonstick baking spray with flour.
2. Grate 1 bar of the bittersweet chocolate and chop the other; set the chopped chocolate aside. In a small bowl, whisk together the grated chocolate and 1 tablespoon of the flour; set aside.
3. In a medium bowl, whisk together the remaining 2 cups flour, the baking powder, and the salt; set aside.
4. In a large bowl using a handheld mixer, beat together the butter and sugar on medium-high speed for 3 to 5 minutes, or until light and fluffy. Beat in the eggs one at a time, beating well after each addition. Beat in the vanilla.
5. With the mixer on low speed, beat in the flour mixture in three additions, alternating with the milk, beginning and ending with the flour.
6. Stir in the grated chocolate mixture by hand.
7. Spoon the batter into the prepared pan. Bake for 50 to 60 minutes, or until a wooden pick inserted into the center comes out clean.

TIP:

Grating the chocolate is what creates the delightful tweed look in this cake. A Microplane rasp grater or the small holes of a box grater can be used to grate the chocolate. Hold the edges of the chocolate bar lightly to avoid melting the chocolate, and if it becomes too warm to grate, place it in the freezer for just a minute or two. Collect any pieces that are too small to hold and grate, and add them to the chocolate that will be melted for the topping. If you do not wish to grate the chocolate, you could evenly chop it; the baked cake may not have the even tweed appearance, but it will still taste luscious.

8. Place the cake on a wire rack to cool for 10 minutes. Invert the cake onto the rack and let cool completely.

9. In a small microwave-safe glass bowl, microwave the chopped chocolate on High (100%) power in 30-second intervals, stirring after each, until the chocolate is melted and smooth. Spoon the melted bittersweet chocolate into a zip-top bag.

10. In a small microwave-safe glass bowl, microwave the white chocolate on High (100%) power in 20-second intervals, stirring after each, until melted and smooth. (Watch carefully to avoid scorching.) Spoon the melted white chocolate into a zip-top bag.

11. Snip off a tiny corner of the bag of bittersweet chocolate. Drizzle about three-quarters of the bittersweet chocolate in narrow straight stripes across the cake. Snip off a tiny corner of the bag of white chocolate. Drizzle about three-quarters of the white chocolate in narrow, straight stripes perpendicular to the bittersweet chocolate stripes to make a crosshatch design. Repeat with the remaining bittersweet chocolate, making straight lines in the same direction as the first bittersweet chocolate lines, then do the same with the remaining white chocolate.

Chocolate Cherry Cordial Bundt Cake

MAKES 1 BUNDT CAKE

Chocolate cherry cordials are a classic candy, and it is no wonder. They are divine, and that sweet cherry, enrobed in chocolate, is a timeless treat. Can you almost taste it? In this Chocolate Cherry Cordial Bundt Cake you will find those same maraschino cherries shining like jewels in a rich chocolate cake, and, of course, the cake is covered in more chocolate. We like to arrange some chocolate cherry cordial candies along the edges of the cake platter as a fun garnish and an extra treat.

Nonstick baking spray with flour

½ cup semisweet chocolate chips

1 (10-ounce) jar stemless maraschino cherries

1 (15.25- to 18-ounce) box chocolate fudge cake mix

⅓ cup vegetable or canola oil

4 large eggs

¼ cup brandy

¼ cup water

Chocolate Ganache (page 147)

TIP:

If desired, substitute ½ cup whole milk for the brandy and water.

1. Preheat the oven to 350°F. Spray a 12-cup Bundt pan with nonstick baking spray with flour.

2. In a small microwave-safe glass bowl, microwave the chocolate chips on High (100%) power in 30-second intervals, stirring well after each, until the chocolate is melted. Stir until smooth and set aside to cool slightly.

3. Drain the maraschino cherries, reserving the juice. Measure out ½ cup of the reserved juice. Pat the cherries dry with a paper towel. Finely chop the cherries and place them in a small bowl. Sprinkle the cherries with 2 tablespoons of the dry cake mix and toss to coat evenly; set aside.

4. In a large bowl using a handheld mixer, blend together the remaining cake mix, oil, eggs, reserved ½ cup maraschino cherry juice, brandy, water, and melted chocolate on low speed. Scrape down the sides of the bowl well and beat on medium speed for 2 minutes. Stir in the cherry mixture.

5. Spoon the batter into the prepared pan. Bake for 45 to 55 minutes, or until a wooden pick inserted into the center comes out clean.

6. Place the cake on a wire rack to cool for 10 minutes. Invert the cake onto the rack and let cool completely.

7. Set the cake on the rack over a sheet of parchment paper to catch any drips and drizzle with the Chocolate Ganache.

Cola Bundt Cake

MAKES 1 BUNDT CAKE

Jell-O salads, ham glazes, and, yes, cakes and frostings are all bound to have cola added to them if you were raised south of the Mason-Dixon Line. Thank goodness! The sweet cola flavor forms a unique syrup that only cola can add. Frosting the finished cake with Cola Icing truly elevates this recipe to five stars.

Nonstick baking spray with flour

1 (15.25- to 18-ounce) box dark chocolate cake mix

2 tablespoons unsweetened cocoa powder

½ cup (1 stick) unsalted butter, melted

1 cup cola

½ cup buttermilk

4 large eggs

1 teaspoon pure vanilla extract

Cola Icing (page 152)

½ coarsely chopped pecans, toasted (see page 12)

1. Preheat the oven to 350°F. Spray a 10-cup Bundt pan with nonstick baking spray with flour.

2. In a large bowl using a handheld mixer, blend together the cake mix, cocoa powder, melted butter, cola, buttermilk, eggs, and vanilla on low speed. Scrape down the sides of the bowl well and beat on medium speed for 2 minutes.

3. Pour the batter into the prepared pan. Bake for 40 to 50 minutes, or until a wooden pick inserted into the center comes out clean.

4. Place the cake on a wire rack to cool for 10 minutes. Invert the cake onto the rack and let cool completely.

5. Set the cake on the rack over a sheet of parchment paper to catch any drips and drizzle with the Cola Icing. Sprinkle evenly with the pecans.

VARIATION:

Cherry Cola Bundt Cake

In a small bowl, stir together ¾ cup dried, pitted cherries and 2 tablespoons cherry liqueur; allow to stand for 10 minutes. Drain and pat the cherries dry. Toss the cherries in 2 tablespoons of the cake mix. Substitute cherry flavored cola for the cola. Prepare the batter as directed, then stir in the dried cherries. Bake as directed. Frost with Cherry Cola Icing (page 152). Omit the pecan garnish.

TIP:

You can use any of your favorite chocolate-flavored cake mixes for this recipe.

Chocolate Mayonnaise Bundt Cake

MAKES 1 BUNDT CAKE

If you are on the hunt for a truly moist chocolate cake, you have found it! Hellmann's, the mayonnaise company, printed the first mayonnaise cake recipe in a cake booklet published in 1937. The rest, as they say, is history. Since mayonnaise has a high oil content, it lends itself as a miraculous ingredient in this cake. No need to use a boxed mix to ensure a moist cake that will keep that moisture for days after it is baked. We think you will agree that this is a "must-have" cake recipe. We adapted this recipe for a Bundt pan from the original Hellmann's recipe.

Nonstick baking spray with flour

2 cups all-purpose flour

$\frac{1}{3}$ cup unsweetened cocoa powder

$1\frac{1}{4}$ teaspoons baking soda

$\frac{1}{4}$ teaspoon baking powder

3 large eggs

$1\frac{1}{3}$ cups granulated sugar

1 teaspoon pure vanilla extract

1 cup mayonnaise (not reduced-fat version)

$1\frac{1}{3}$ cups water

Confectioners' sugar, for garnish

TIP:

This cake is delicious with a frosting or glaze. Omit the confectioners' sugar and drizzle with Chocolate Frosting (page 146) or Rich Cream Glaze (page 143) instead

1. Preheat the oven to 350°F. Spray a 10-cup Bundt pan with nonstick baking spray with flour.
2. In a medium bowl, whisk together the flour, cocoa powder, baking soda, and baking powder; set aside.
3. In a large bowl using a handheld mixer, beat together the eggs, granulated sugar, and vanilla on medium-high speed for about 3 minutes, until light and fluffy. Add the mayonnaise and blend until smooth.
4. With the mixer on low speed, beat in the flour mixture in three additions, alternating with the water, beginning and ending with the flour.
5. Pour the batter into the prepared pan. Bake for 35 to 45 minutes, or until a wooden pick inserted into the center comes out clean.
6. Place the cake on a wire rack to cool for 10 minutes. Invert the cake onto the rack and let cool completely.
7. Dust with confectioners' sugar.

POUND AND COFFEE CAKES

Southern Pound Bundt Cake

MAKES 1 BUNDT CAKE

Pound cake, a Southern staple, can be worth its weight in gold. When you try this recipe, it will all make sense, and you will discover what Southerners have known all along. Heaven! This is great on its own, but it is over the top when fresh peaches, dripping with juice, are spooned over the top. For that matter, any fresh, in-season fruit would be delicious served with this cake.

Nonstick baking spray with flour

2¾ cups all-purpose flour

1 teaspoon salt

1½ cups (3 sticks) unsalted butter, softened

2¾ cups granulated sugar

4 ounces cream cheese, softened

5 large eggs

¼ cup whole milk

1 teaspoon pure vanilla extract

1 teaspoon almond extract

Confectioners' sugar, for garnish

VARIATION:

Golden Maple Pecan Pound Bundt Cake
Substitute maple extract for the almond extract. Prepare the batter as directed. Stir in ½ cup chopped, toasted pecans. Bake as directed. Omit the confectioners' sugar. Frost with Maple Frosting (page 152).

1. Preheat the oven to 300°F. Spray a 12-cup Bundt pan with nonstick baking spray with flour.
2. In a medium bowl, stir together the flour and salt; set aside.
3. In the bowl of a stand mixer fitted with the paddle attachment, beat together the butter, granulated sugar, and cream cheese on medium-high speed for 5 minutes, until fluffy and pale. Beat in the eggs one at a time, beating well after each addition. Add the milk, vanilla, and almond extract and beat well.
4. With the mixer on low speed, beat in the flour mixture in three additions, blending well and scraping down the sides of the bowl after each addition.
5. Spoon the batter into the prepared pan. Bake for 1 hour 20 minutes to 1 hour 30 minutes, or until a wooden pick inserted into the center comes out clean.

6. Place the cake on a wire rack to cool for 15 minutes. Invert the cake onto the rack and let cool completely.
7. Set the cake on the rack over a sheet of parchment paper and dust with confectioners' sugar.

SIDE NOTE:

Bundt cakes make delicious cupcake-size Bundt cakes (often called Bundtlettes) or small cakes. Spray the pan with nonstick baking spray with flour, then fill the pan about ½ to ¾ full with batter. Bake, using the oven temperature stated in the recipe, but reduce the baking time. Generally begin checking for doneness after about 15 minutes, then watch carefully to avoid over baking. Bake the cake until a wooden pick inserted in the center comes out clean.

Sour Cream Chocolate Pound Bundt Cake

MAKES 1 BUNDT CAKE

The sour cream in this Sour Cream Chocolate Pound Bundt Cake keeps the cake moist, and the combination of semisweet chocolate and cocoa gives it the perfect balance of chocolate. This versatile chocolate cake is kind of like that little black dress you can wear anywhere. It is perfect as is, or you can top a piece with a scoop of vanilla ice cream or spoonfuls of fresh raspberries or strawberries and a dollop of whipped cream for a memorable dessert. And just like you wear that little black dress often, you will find lots of reasons to bake this cake.

Nonstick baking spray with flour
1 (4-ounce) bar semisweet chocolate, chopped
½ cup unsweetened cocoa powder
1 teaspoon instant espresso powder
½ cup boiling water
1¼ cups all-purpose flour
1 teaspoon baking soda
¼ teaspoon baking powder
½ teaspoon salt
½ cup (1 stick) unsalted butter, softened
2 tablespoons vegetable or canola oil
1 cup packed brown sugar
⅓ cup granulated sugar
3 large eggs
¾ cup sour cream
2 teaspoons pure vanilla extract
Chocolate Glaze (page 146)

1. Preheat the oven to 325°F. Spray a 10-cup Bundt pan with nonstick baking spray with flour.
2. In a small bowl, combine the chopped chocolate, cocoa powder, and espresso powder. Pour the boiling water over the mixture and let stand for 2 to 3 minutes so the chocolate melts. Whisk until smooth. Set aside to cool completely.
3. In a medium bowl, whisk together the flour, baking soda, baking powder, and salt; set aside.

4. In a large bowl using a handheld mixer, beat together the butter, oil, brown sugar, and granulated sugar on medium-high speed for 3 to 5 minutes, or until light and fluffy. Beat in the eggs, one a time, beating well after each addition. Beat in the sour cream and the vanilla.

5. With the mixer on low speed, beat in the flour mixture in three additions, alternating with the chocolate mixture, beginning and ending with the flour mixture and blending until just combined.

6. Spoon the batter into the prepared pan. Bake for 35 to 45 minutes or until a wooden pick inserted into the center comes out clean.

7. Place the cake on a wire rack to cool for 10 minutes. Invert the cake onto the rack and let cool completely.

8. Set the cake on the rack over a sheet of parchment paper to catch any drips and drizzle with the Chocolate Glaze.

Spice Pound Bundt Cake

MAKES 1 BUNDT CAKE

Do you need a go-to recipe for football tailgating? Here is the answer. This one-bowl Spice Pound Bundt Cake with Maple Frosting comes together in a snap and will be a winner, no matter which team comes out on top.

Nonstick baking spray with flour
2½ cups all-purpose flour
1½ cups packed brown sugar
2 teaspoons baking powder
½ teaspoon baking soda
½ teaspoon salt
1½ teaspoons ground cinnamon
1 teaspoon ground ginger
¼ teaspoon ground nutmeg
¼ teaspoon ground cloves
¼ teaspoon ground allspice
4 large eggs
1¼ cups sour cream
¾ cup (1½ sticks) unsalted butter, softened
1 teaspoon pure vanilla extract
Maple Frosting (page 152)

TIP:

If desired, you can eliminate the cinnamon, ginger, nutmeg, cloves, and allspice and substitute 3¼ teaspoons pumpkin pie spice.

1. Preheat the oven to 350°F. Spray a 10-cup Bundt pan with nonstick baking spray with flour.
2. In a large bowl, whisk together the flour, brown sugar, baking powder, baking soda, salt, cinnamon, ginger, nutmeg, cloves, and allspice.
3. Add the eggs, sour cream, butter, and vanilla to the flour mixture and use a handheld mixer on low speed to blend well. Scrape down the sides of the bowl and beat on medium speed for 2 minutes.
4. Pour the batter into the prepared pan. Bake for 45 to 55 minutes, or until a wooden pick inserted into the center comes out clean.
5. Place the cake on a wire rack to cool for 10 minutes. Invert the cake onto the rack and let cool completely.
6. Frost the cooled cake with the Maple Frosting.

Honey Bee Bundt Cake

MAKES 1 BUNDT CAKE

Do you dream of going on a picnic like all those beautiful magazine pictures portray? Or are you packing lunches and want a treat that transports easily? Either way, this Honey Bee Bundt Cake fills the bill and tastes great. It is a dense cake, similar to a pound cake, but one that is lightly sweetened with honey and flavored with a touch of ginger. The honey glaze you brush over the cake after baking seeps into the cake, adding even more flavor. If you want to really dress it up, serve each slice of cake with fresh berries or orange segments and top it with a dollop of whipped cream.

Nonstick baking spray with flour
2⅓ cups all-purpose flour
1 teaspoon baking powder
½ teaspoon baking soda
½ teaspoon salt
2 tablespoons minced crystallized ginger
Grated zest of 1 lemon
⅓ cup vegetable or canola oil
¾ cup honey
⅓ cup granulated sugar
½ cup packed brown sugar
2 tablespoons fresh lemon juice
2 large eggs
1 cup whole milk

Honey Glaze

4 tablespoons (½ stick) unsalted butter
¼ cup honey
3 tablespoons packed brown sugar
1 tablespoon fresh lemon juice
1 tablespoon heavy cream

TIP:

Crystallized ginger is readily available in most grocery stores and is usually found with the spices and seasonings. The soft pieces of ginger have been candied so they are lightly sweetened and easy to chop with a sharp knife.

When measuring honey, or any sticky ingredient, first spray the measuring cup with nonstick cooking spray. This will make it much easier to get all the honey out of the cup.

1. Preheat the oven to 350°F. Spray a 10-cup Bundt pan with nonstick baking spray with flour.
2. In a medium bowl, whisk together the flour, baking powder, baking soda, salt, ginger, and lemon zest; set aside.

3. In large bowl using a handheld mixer, blend together the oil, honey, granulated sugar, and brown sugar on medium speed. Add the lemon juice and beat for 1 minute. Beat in the eggs, one at a time, beating well after each addition.

4. With the mixer on low speed, beat in the flour mixture in three additions, alternating with the milk, beginning and ending with the flour.

5. Pour the batter into the prepared pan. Bake for 45 to 55 minutes, or until a wooden pick inserted into the center comes out clean.

6. Place the cake on a wire rack to cool for 10 minutes. Invert the cake onto the rack and let cool completely.

7. Meanwhile, make the Honey Glaze: In a microwave-safe 2-cup glass measuring cup or bowl, microwave the butter on High (100%) power for 30 to 40 seconds, or until melted. Stir in the honey and brown sugar and microwave on High (100%) power for 15 seconds, or until bubbling. Stir until the sugar has dissolved. Stir in the lemon juice and heavy cream.

8. Set the cake on the rack over a sheet of parchment paper to catch any drips. Using a skewer, poke holes over the top of the cake. Using a pastry brush, brush the warm Honey Glaze over the top and sides of the cake, filling all the holes, then drizzle the remaining glaze over the top of the cake.

Snickerdoodle Coffee Cake

MAKES 1 BUNDT CAKE

No need to wait until April 7, National Coffee Cake Day, to enjoy a slice of deliciousness. Coffee cakes are believed to have originated in Europe and traveled to the United States during the 1700s. They tasted more like bread in the early days, but evolved into a cake with a streusel filling or topping. Today, no breakfast or brunch menu would be complete without a coffee cake.

Nonstick baking spray with flour
⅓ cup packed brown sugar
⅓ cup granulated sugar
1 tablespoon ground cinnamon
1 (15.25- to 18-ounce) box yellow cake mix
1 (3.4-ounce) box vanilla instant pudding mix
4 large eggs
¾ cup buttermilk
½ cup vegetable or canola oil
½ cup sour cream

TIP:

If desired, add ½ cup chopped toasted pecans or walnuts to the cinnamon-sugar mixture (see page 12 for instructions on toasting nuts); proceed as directed.

1. Preheat the oven to 350°F. Spray a 10-cup Bundt pan with nonstick baking spray with flour.
2. In a small bowl, stir together the brown sugar, granulated sugar, and cinnamon; set aside.
3. In a large bowl using a handheld mixer, blend together the cake mix, pudding mix, eggs, buttermilk, oil, and sour cream. Scrape down the sides of the bowl well and beat on medium speed for 2 minutes.
4. Pour half the batter into the prepared pan. Sprinkle with two-thirds of the cinnamon-sugar mixture. Pour the remaining batter over the top and spread it evenly. Sprinkle the top of the cake with the remaining cinnamon-sugar mixture.
5. Bake for 35 to 45 minutes, or until a wooden pick inserted into the center comes out clean.
6. Place the cake on a wire rack to cool for 10 minutes. Invert the cake onto a serving platter, being careful to allow the platter to "catch" any loose cinnamon sugar. Serve warm or at room temperature.

Banana-Walnut Bundt Coffee Cake

MAKES 1 BUNDT CAKE

The last food that we would call a "fad" or mention as a trend is a moist and flavorful banana bread or banana cake. It is a taste of home, and perhaps nothing tastes more comforting. Yet it seems that more and more bakeries and coffee shops are offering a thick slice to go with cups of coffee or tea. It is a delicious combo, but why go out? The unbeatable banana flavor in this Banana-Walnut Bundt Coffee Cake is accented with nuggets of walnuts, and the Brown Sugar Glaze adds pure bliss to every bite.

Nonstick baking spray with flour
2 cups all-purpose flour
1 teaspoon baking soda
½ teaspoon baking powder
½ teaspoon salt
½ cup (1 stick) unsalted butter, softened
½ cup granulated sugar
½ cup packed brown sugar
2 large eggs
1 teaspoon pure vanilla extract
3 ripe medium bananas, mashed
1 cup buttermilk
½ cup chopped walnuts, toasted (see page 12)
Brown Sugar Glaze (page 151)

VARIATION:

Chocolate-Banana Bundt Coffee Cake Prepare the batter as directed. Stir in ½ cup mini chocolate chips. Bake as directed. Drizzle with Chocolate Glaze (page 146) instead of the Brown Sugar Glaze.

TIP:

Toasting the walnuts intensifies their flavor (see page 12 for instructions on toasting nuts).

1. Preheat the oven to 350°F. Spray a 10-cup Bundt pan with nonstick baking spray with flour.
2. In a medium bowl, whisk together the flour, baking soda, baking powder, and salt; set aside.
3. In a large bowl using a handheld mixer, beat together the butter, granulated sugar, and brown sugar on medium-high speed for 3 to 5 minutes, or until light and fluffy. Beat in the eggs one a time, beating well after each addition. Beat in the vanilla and mashed bananas.
4. With the mixer on low speed, beat in the flour mixture in three additions, alternating with the buttermilk, beginning and ending with the flour and mixing just until blended. Stir in the walnuts by hand.

5. Spoon the batter into the prepared pan. Bake for 40 to 50 minutes, or until a wooden pick inserted into the center comes out clean.
6. Place the cake on a wire rack to cool for 10 minutes. Invert the cake onto the rack and let cool completely.
7. Set the cake on the rack over a sheet of parchment paper to catch any drips and drizzle with the Brown Sugar Glaze.

Blueberry Yogurt Coffee Cake

MAKES 1 BUNDT CAKE

The yogurt-and-blueberry goodness of this Blueberry Yogurt Coffee Cake sets it several bars ahead of ho-hum coffee cake. This recipe provides a wonderful excuse to invite friends over for Sunday brunch. No worries, and entertaining is a breeze.

Nonstick baking spray with flour
1¾ cups plus 1 tablespoon all-purpose flour
1½ teaspoons baking powder
½ teaspoon salt
2 cups fresh blueberries
1 cup (2 sticks) unsalted butter, softened
2 cups granulated sugar
2 large eggs
1 cup plain Greek yogurt
1 teaspoon pure vanilla extract
Confectioners' sugar, for garnish (optional)

Brown Sugar Streusel
½ cup packed brown sugar
1 teaspoon ground cinnamon
½ cup chopped pecans, toasted (see page 12)

TIPS:

You can use 2 cups frozen blueberries in place of the fresh. Do not thaw the berries. Toss the frozen berries with the 1 tablespoon flour as directed in the recipe.

You can substitute 1 cup sour cream for the yogurt.

1. Preheat the oven to 350°F. Spray a 10-cup Bundt pan with nonstick baking spray with flour.
2. Make the Brown Sugar Streusel: In a small bowl, stir together the brown sugar, cinnamon, and pecans; set aside.
3. In a medium bowl, whisk together 1¾ cups of the flour, the baking powder, and the salt; set aside.
4. In a medium bowl, toss the blueberries with the remaining 1 tablespoon flour; set aside.
5. In a large bowl using a handheld mixer, beat together the butter and granulated sugar on medium-high speed for 3 to 5 minutes, or until light and fluffy. Beat in the eggs one at a time, beating well after each addition. Beat in the yogurt and vanilla; do not overmix.

6. Stir the flour mixture into the batter by hand until just blended. Gently fold the blueberry mixture into the batter.

7. Spoon half the batter into the prepared pan. Sprinkle half the Brown Sugar Streusel over the batter in the pan. Top with the remaining batter and sprinkle with the remaining streusel. Gently draw a butter knife through the batter to create a marbled effect (do not overblend—the batter and streusel should remain distinct).

8. Bake for 60 to 70 minutes, or until a wooden pick inserted near the center comes out clean.

9. Place the cake on a wire rack to cool for 15 minutes. Invert the cake onto a serving platter and let cool completely.

10. Dust with confectioners' sugar before serving.

11. Store in an airtight container to keep fresh for up to 5 days.

Overnight Caramel Cinnamon Roll Bundt Cake

MAKES 1 BUNDT CAKE

We are not trying to pull the wool over your eyes. This technically is not a cake, but it does use a Bundt pan, and it is so easy to prepare when you have overnight guests. It is addicting and delicious, and if truth be told, you won't want wait to make this until you have overnight guests. It will make any Sunday brunch a success!

Nonstick cooking spray
½ cup chopped pecans, toasted (see page 12)
20 frozen dinner rolls (do not thaw)
1 (3.4-ounce) box butterscotch instant pudding mix
½ cup (1 stick) unsalted butter, cut into cubes
¾ cup packed brown sugar
1½ teaspoons ground cinnamon

1. Spray a 15-cup Bundt pan with nonstick cooking spray. Sprinkle the nuts evenly over the bottom of the pan. Place the frozen dinner rolls evenly into the pan. Sprinkle the pudding mix evenly over the rolls.
2. In a small saucepan, combine the butter, brown sugar, and cinnamon. Bring to a simmer over medium-high heat, stirring frequently; remove from the heat and pour evenly into the pan. Cover with plastic wrap and allow to stand at room temperature overnight.
3. When ready to bake, preheat the oven to 350°F.
4. Bake for 25 to 35 minutes. Using hot pads, carefully invert the Bundt pan onto a platter with short sides (so the delicious caramel won't run onto the counter). Serve warm.

Butter Pecan Coffee Cake

MAKES 1 BUNDT CAKE

Do you ever pick up a coffee cake at the grocery store bakery? Or maybe you have hunted the frozen food aisle for a particular frozen coffee cake. Well, no more. This Butter Pecan Coffee Cake is, just as the name says, a buttery coffee cake laced with pecans and a touch of cinnamon. It comes together in a jiffy and tastes so much better than those store-bought options.

Nonstick baking spray with flour
1 (15.25- to 18-ounce) box yellow cake mix
1 (3.4-ounce) box vanilla instant pudding mix
½ cup (1 stick) unsalted butter, softened
¾ cup water
4 large eggs
2 teaspoons butter extract
1 teaspoon pure vanilla extract
Vanilla Glaze (page 142)
Pecan halves, toasted (see page 12), for garnish (optional)

Pecan Streusel
⅓ cup granulated sugar
⅓ cup packed brown sugar
¾ cup chopped pecans, toasted (see page 12)
1 tablespoon ground cinnamon

1. Preheat the oven to 350°F. Spray a 12-cup Bundt pan with nonstick baking spray with flour.
2. Make the Pecan Streusel: In a small bowl, stir together the granulated sugar, brown sugar, pecans, and cinnamon; set aside.
3. In a large bowl using a handheld mixer, blend together the cake mix, pudding mix, butter, water, eggs, butter extract, and vanilla on low speed. Scrape down the sides of the bowl well and beat on medium speed for 2 minutes.

4. Pour about one-third of the batter into the prepared pan. Sprinkle with half the Pecan Streusel. Top with another third of the batter, then sprinkle with the remaining Pecan Streusel. Top with the remaining batter, spreading it evenly.
5. Bake for 35 to 45 minutes, or until a wooden pick inserted into the center comes out clean.
6. Place the cake on a wire rack to cool for 10 minutes. Invert the cake onto the rack and let cool completely.
7. Set the cake on the rack over a sheet of parchment paper to catch any drips and drizzle with the Vanilla Glaze. Garnish with pecan halves, if desired.

VARIATIONS:

Chocolate Pecan Streusel Coffee Cake

Substitute chocolate cake mix for the yellow cake mix and chocolate instant pudding mix for the vanilla. Omit the butter extract. Prepare the cake with the Pecan Streusel as directed, then bake as directed. Glaze with Chocolate Glaze (page 146) and garnish with pecan halves.

MARBLES, TUNNELS, SWIRLS, AND FILLED BUNDT CAKES

Vanilla Cream Bundt Cake

MAKES 1 BUNDT CAKE

We have been blessed to work together, cooking and baking, for more than three decades! All our clients and projects have been memorable and fun, but perhaps none as memorable as the time we tested all the recipes for The Twinkies Cookbook. *This recipe for Vanilla Cream Bundt Cake has been adapted from one we tested for that cookbook and labeled a winner.*

Nonstick baking spray with flour
1 (15.25- to 18-ounce) box devil's food or chocolate cake mix
1 (3.9-ounce) box chocolate instant pudding mix
1 cup sour cream
½ cup water
4 large eggs
5 Twinkies, cut in half crosswise
Chocolate Frosting (page 146)

TIP:

The Vanilla Cream Bundt cake can be prepared with any flavor of cake mix that you prefer. You can frost it with a white or chocolate frosting, or you may decide not to frost it at all. Any of these choices produces a delicious cake!

1. Preheat the oven to 350°F. Spray a 10-cup Bundt pan with nonstick baking spray with flour.
2. In a large bowl using a handheld mixer, blend together the cake mix, pudding mix, sour cream, water, and eggs on low speed. Scrape down the sides of the bowl well and beat on medium speed for 2 minutes.
3. Pour half the batter into the prepared pan. Place the Twinkies evenly into the batter around the pan, cut-side down. Pour the remaining batter over the Twinkies. Use a spatula if needed to cover the Twinkies with the batter.
4. Bake for 50 to 60 minutes, or until a wooden pick inserted into the center (not touching a filled Twinkie) comes out clean.
5. Place the cake on a wire rack to cool for 10 minutes. Invert the cake onto the rack and let cool completely.
6. Spread the Chocolate Frosting over the top of the cake.

Red Velvet Marble Bundt Cake

MAKES 1 BUNDT CAKE

Some friends have in-your-face personalities, while others are more subdued but equally intriguing. We think you'll agree that a blend of friendships makes for a fuller life. The same is true with cake. Some folks adore the vibrant red of a true red velvet cake, while others savor and linger over red velvet marble. Don't judge; just make room for both in your baking repertoire. Life and baking are about balance.

Nonstick baking spray with flour

3¼ cups all-purpose flour

1½ teaspoons baking soda

¾ cup (1½ sticks) unsalted butter, softened

⅓ cup vegetable shortening

2¼ cups granulated sugar

5 large eggs

4 teaspoons white vinegar

1½ teaspoons pure vanilla extract

1½ cups buttermilk

3 tablespoons unsweetened cocoa powder

4½ teaspoons red food coloring

Vanilla Glaze (page 142)

Coarse red sparkling sugar, for garnish

TIP:

This is also good with Cream Cheese Glaze (page 143). If glazed with Cream Cheese Glaze, store the cake in an airtight container in the refrigerator.

1. Preheat the oven to 325°F. Spray a 15-cup Bundt pan with nonstick baking spray with flour.
2. In a medium bowl, whisk together the flour and baking soda; set aside.
3. In the bowl of a stand mixer fitted with the paddle attachment, beat together the butter, shortening, and granulated sugar on medium-high speed for 3 to 5 minutes, or until light and fluffy. Beat in the eggs one at a time, beating well after each addition. Beat in the vinegar and vanilla.
4. With the mixer on low speed, beat in the flour mixture in three additions, alternating with the buttermilk, beginning and ending with the flour mixture.
5. Transfer half the batter to another bowl. Stir in the cocoa powder and red food coloring; blend well.

6. Spoon half the butter batter into the prepared pan and spread it evenly. Dollop with half the red batter and spread it evenly over the butter batter. Repeat the layers, using the remaining batter.

7. Bake 60 to 70 minutes, or until a wooden pick inserted into the center comes out clean.

8. Place the cake on a wire rack to cool for 10 minutes. Invert the cake onto the rack and let cool completely.

9. Set the cake on the rack over a sheet of parchment paper to catch any drips and drizzle with Vanilla Glaze. Sprinkle with red sparkling sugar.

10. Store any leftovers at room temperature in an airtight container.

Chocolate Peanut Butter Tunnel Bundt Cake

MAKES 1 BUNDT CAKE

Chocolate and peanut butter are meant to be married into a terrific flavor combo. If you crave those famous chocolate peanut butter cups, then this recipe is for you. Kids and adults alike will enjoy this cake. You can take it up a notch by serving a slice with a scoop of vanilla ice cream on top and then adding a drizzle of chocolate syrup.

Nonstick baking spray with flour

1 (15.25- to 18-ounce) box milk chocolate cake mix

½ cup vegetable or canola oil

½ cup water

½ cup sour cream

4 large eggs

1 teaspoon pure vanilla extract

²/₃ cup peanut butter chips

Chocolate Glaze (page 146)

Peanut Butter Filling

¾ cup creamy peanut butter

4 ounces cream cheese, softened

¼ cup confectioners' sugar, sifted

1 large egg

3 tablespoons whole milk

Peanut Butter Tunnel Bundt Glaze

1 cup peanut butter chips

⅓ cup heavy cream

TIP:

One (10-ounce) package peanut butter chips is ideally sized for the cake and peanut butter glaze, giving you just enough chips for both.

1. Preheat the oven to 350°F. Spray a 12-cup Bundt pan with nonstick baking spray with flour.
2. Make the Peanut Butter Filling: In a medium bowl using a handheld mixer, beat together the peanut butter, cream cheese, confectioners' sugar, egg, and milk on medium speed until smooth; set aside.

3. Make the Cake: In a large bowl using a handheld mixer, blend together the cake mix, oil, water, sour cream, eggs, and vanilla on low speed. Scrape down the sides of the bowl well and beat on medium speed for 2 minutes.

4. Measure out 2 cups of the batter and set aside. Pour the remaining batter into the prepared pan. Using a teaspoon, dollop the Peanut Butter Filling on top of the batter in the pan, mounding it into a narrow stripe not touching the sides of the pan. Sprinkle $1/3$ cup of the peanut butter chips on top of the peanut butter filling stripe. Pour the remaining chocolate batter evenly over the Peanut Butter Filling, covering it completely.

5. Bake for 45 to 55 minutes, or until the cake begins to pull away from the sides of the pan and the center springs back when you touch it lightly. (You can not test for doneness with a wooden pick because the cake has a filling.)

6. Place the cake on a wire rack to cool for 10 minutes. Invert the cake onto the rack and let cool completely.

7. Meanwhile, make the Peanut Butter Glaze: In a small microwave-safe glass bowl, microwave the peanut butter chips and cream on High (100%) power for 30 seconds; stir until smooth. If needed, microwave for 15 seconds more, until the chips are melted.

8. Set the cake on the rack over a sheet of parchment paper to catch any drips and drizzle the Peanut Butter Glaze over the cooled cake. Drizzle the Chocolate Glaze over the Peanut Butter Glaze in a decorative manner.

9. Store the cake in the refrigerator until ready to serve. Keep any leftovers refrigerated.

Chocolate–Coconut Macaroon Bundt Cake

MAKES 1 BUNDT CAKE

Coconut macaroons are wonderful, chewy coconut cookies. Now imagine those coconut delights enrobed in milk chocolate, and you have the inspiration for this delicious Chocolate–Coconut Macaroon Bundt Cake.

Nonstick baking spray with flour
¾ cup milk chocolate chips
1 cup (2 sticks) unsalted butter
⅓ cup unsweetened cocoa powder
⅓ cup water
2⅓ cups all-purpose flour
1¾ cups granulated sugar
1½ teaspoons baking soda
½ teaspoon salt
¾ cup sour cream
2 large eggs
1 large egg yolk
1 teaspoon pure vanilla extract
Milk Chocolate Glaze (page 147)
Sweetened flaked coconut, for garnish (optional)

Coconut Filling

½ cup confectioners' sugar
1 tablespoon all-purpose flour
1½ cups sweetened flaked coconut
1 large egg white
1 teaspoon pure vanilla extract

TIP:

One (12-ounce) bag of milk chocolate chips is ideally sized for this cake and glaze, giving you just enough chips for both.

1. Preheat the oven to 350°F. Spray a 15-cup Bundt pan with nonstick baking spray with flour.
2. Make the Coconut Filling: In a medium bowl, stir together the confectioners' sugar and flour. Stir in the coconut, egg white, and vanilla and blend until the coconut is evenly coated; set aside.

3. Make the Cake: In a small saucepan, melt the chocolate chips and the butter over low heat. Stir in the cocoa powder and water. Heat, stirring continuously, until blended and smooth. Remove from the heat and allow to cool for 10 minutes.

4. In a large bowl, whisk together the flour, granulated sugar, baking soda, and salt. Add the chocolate mixture, sour cream, eggs, egg yolk, and vanilla and use a handheld mixer on medium speed to blend until smooth.

5. Pour about three-quarters of the batter into the prepared pan. Using a teaspoon, dollop the Coconut Filling on top of the batter in the pan, mounding it into a narrow stripe not touching the sides of the pan. Pour the remaining chocolate batter evenly over the Coconut Filling, covering it completely.

6. Bake for 50 to 60 minutes, or until the cake begins to pull away from the sides of the pan and the center springs back when touched lightly. (You cannot test for doneness with a wooden pick as the cake has a coconut center.)

7. Place the cake on a wire rack to cool for 10 minutes. Invert the cake onto the rack and let cool completely.

8. Set the cake on the rack over a sheet of parchment paper to catch any drips and drizzle the Milk Chocolate Glaze over the cake. Garnish with flaked coconut, if desired.

9. Store the cake in the refrigerator until ready to serve. Keep any leftovers refrigerated.

VARIATIONS:

Almond-Coconut Bundt Cake

Prepare and bake the cake according to the directions. Prepare the Milk Chocolate Glaze. Using a drop of chocolate glaze for each as "glue," position 7 to 9 whole almonds around the top of the baked Bundt cake. Gently pour the remaining glaze over the cake, covering the almonds.

Citrus Marble Bundt Cake

MAKES 1 BUNDT CAKE

The bright and clean flavors of orange, lemon, and lime combine in each delicious bite of this Citrus Marble Bundt Cake. The distinctive swirls of color make this a special cake to serve for a shower or tea, and the fact that it doesn't need frosting will make this an ideal treat to pack in a picnic basket or serve on a warm summer day.

Nonstick baking spray with flour

2¾ cups all-purpose flour

1½ teaspoons baking powder

½ teaspoon baking soda

¼ teaspoon salt

1 cup (2 sticks) unsalted butter, softened

2 cups granulated sugar

5 large eggs

6 tablespoons whole milk

Grated zest of 1 orange

2 tablespoons orange juice

Yellow and red food coloring

Grated zest of 1 lemon

2 tablespoons fresh lemon juice

Grated zest of 1 lime

2 tablespoons fresh lime juice

Green food coloring

Orange Glaze (page 145)

TIP:

Food coloring makes the marbled look of the three citrus flavors fun and more clearly reveals that you will be enjoying three distinct flavors in every bite. Of course, the cake will taste just as good if you omit the food coloring from one or all of the flavors.

1. Preheat the oven to 325°F. Spray a 15-cup Bundt pan with nonstick baking spray with flour.
2. In a medium bowl, whisk together the flour, baking powder, baking soda, and salt; set aside.
3. In a large bowl using a handheld mixer, beat together the butter and sugar on medium-high speed for 3 to 5 minutes, or until very light and fluffy. Beat in the eggs one at a time, beating well after each addition.
4. With the mixer on low speed, beat in the flour mixture in three additions, alternating with the milk, beginning and ending with the flour.

5. Spoon 2 cups of the batter into a small bowl. Stir in the orange zest and the orange juice and tint the batter orange using 4 to 6 drops of yellow food coloring and 2 to 3 drops of red food coloring; set aside.

6. Spoon 2 cups of the remaining batter into a small bowl. Stir in the lemon zest and the lemon juice and tint the batter yellow using 5 or 6 drops of yellow food coloring; set aside.

7. Stir the lime zest and lime juice into the remaining batter in the large bowl. Tint the batter pale green with 3 or 4 drops green food coloring.

8. Spoon the batter into the prepared pan, alternating spoonfuls of each flavor of batter. Gently draw a butter knife through the batter to create a marbled effect (do not overmix—the individual colors should remain distinct).

9. Bake for 45 to 55 minutes, or until a wooden pick inserted into the center comes out clean.

10. Place the cake on a wire rack set over a sheet of parchment paper to cool for 10 minutes. While the cake is still in the pan, use a skewer to poke holes in the cake.

11. Pour half the Orange Glaze over the cake, then immediately invert the cake onto a serving platter. Poke holes in the top of the cake with the skewer and pour the remaining Orange Glaze over the top. Allow the cake to cool.

VARIATIONS:

Lemon-Lime Bundt Cake

Omit the orange zest and juice and the red food coloring. Prepare the batter as directed, then divide the batter in half. Stir the lemon zest and 3 tablespoons lemon juice into one half of the batter, and tint it yellow. Stir the lime zest and 3 tablespoons lime juice into the remaining half of the batter and tint it green. Alternately spoon the batter into the pan, then bake as directed. Cool the cake completely. Glaze with Lemon Glaze (page 144) instead of the Orange Glaze.

Chocolate Cheesecake Tunnel Bundt Cake

MAKES 1 BUNDT CAKE

Some decisions are hard. When offered dessert in a restaurant, do you choose cheesecake, or would you prefer a slice of rich chocolate cake? Chocolate Cheesecake Tunnel Bundt Cake erases that struggle so you can enjoy both flavors at once.

Nonstick baking spray with flour
1 (15.25- to 18-ounce) box devil's food cake mix
2 tablespoons unsweetened cocoa powder
4 large eggs
½ cup vegetable or canola oil
¾ cup cold strong brewed coffee
Cream Cheese Glaze (page 143)

Cheesecake Filling

1 (8-ounce) package cream cheese, at room temperature
6 tablespoons granulated sugar
1 tablespoon all-purpose flour
1 large egg
1 teaspoon pure vanilla extract

1. Preheat the oven to 325°F. Spray a 15-cup Bundt pan with nonstick baking spray with flour.
2. Make the Cheesecake Filling: In a medium bowl using a handheld mixer, beat the cream cheese on medium speed until smooth. Add the sugar, flour, egg, and vanilla and beat until smooth; set aside.
3. Make the Cake: In a large bowl using a handheld mixer, blend together the cake mix, cocoa powder, eggs, oil, and coffee on low speed. Scrape down the sides of the bowl well and beat on medium speed for 2 minutes.
4. Spoon about three-quarters of the batter into the prepared pan. Using a teaspoon, dollop the Cheesecake Filling on top of the batter in the Bundt pan, mounding it into a narrow stripe not touching the sides of the pan. Pour the remaining chocolate batter evenly over the Cheesecake Filling, covering it completely.

5. Bake for 45 to 55 minutes, or until the cake begins to pull away from the sides of the pan and the center springs back when touched lightly. (You cannot test for doneness with a wooden pick as the cake has a cream cheese filling.)

6. Place the cake on a wire rack to cool for 10 minutes. Invert the cake onto the rack and let cool completely.

7. Set the cake on the rack over a sheet of parchment paper to catch any drips and drizzle with the Cream Cheese Glaze.

8. Store the cake in the refrigerator until ready to serve. Keep any leftovers refrigerated.

Pumpkin Bundt Cake with Ginger Swirl

MAKES 1 BUNDT CAKE

The first fall day a cool breeze blows, pumpkin seems to become the flavor of the day. We can't argue with that, but this Pumpkin Bundt Cake with Ginger Swirl stands head and shoulders above the rest. Begin with a moist pumpkin cake, then add a beautiful and flavorful ginger-and-spice-laced swirl, and you are set for a real taste treat.

Nonstick baking spray with flour
1 (15.25- to 18-ounce) box yellow cake mix
1 (3.4-ounce) box vanilla instant pudding mix
1 cup pure pumpkin puree
½ cup vegetable or canola oil
½ cup whole milk
4 large eggs
1 teaspoon ground ginger
½ teaspoon ground cinnamon
¼ teaspoon ground cloves
Cream Cheese Glaze (page 143)

VARIATION:

Sweet Potato Bundt Cake with Ginger Swirl
Substitute cooked, mashed sweet potatoes for the pumpkin. Prepare and bake the cake as directed.

TIP:

Leftover canned pumpkin? Refrigerate the pumpkin in a covered container for up to 1 week or freeze for up to 3 months. When ready to use, thaw the pumpkin overnight in the refrigerator, then stir well and use as desired.

1. Preheat the oven to 350°F. Spray a 12-cup Bundt pan with nonstick baking spray with flour.
2. In a large bowl using a handheld mixer, blend together the cake mix, pudding mix, pumpkin puree, oil, milk, and eggs on low speed. Scrape down the sides of the bowl well and beat on medium speed for 2 minutes.
3. Spoon 1 cup of the batter into a small bowl. Stir in the ginger, cinnamon, and cloves; set aside.
4. Spoon three-quarters of the pumpkin batter into the prepared pan. Spoon the ginger swirl batter over the pumpkin batter in the pan. Top with the remaining pumpkin batter. Gently draw a butter knife through the batter to create a marbled effect (do not overblend—the pumpkin and ginger batters should remain distinct).
5. Bake for 40 to 50 minutes, or until a wooden pick inserted into the center comes out clean.
6. Place the cake on a wire rack to cool for 10 minutes. Invert the cake onto the rack and let cool completely.

7. Set the cake on the rack over a sheet of parchment paper to catch any drips and drizzle with the Cream Cheese Glaze.

8. Store the cake in the refrigerator until ready to serve. Keep any leftovers refrigerated.

Chocolate Whoopie Bundt Cake

MAKES 1 BUNDT CAKE

Individual whoopie pies can be time consuming and, honestly, a hassle to prepare. No need to worry about that anymore—the answer is to make one large Chocolate Whoopie Bundt Cake and enjoy.

Nonstick baking spray with flour
1 (15.25- to 18-ounce) box chocolate fudge cake mix
1 (3.9-ounce) box chocolate instant pudding mix
1 cup sour cream
½ cup whole milk
½ cup vegetable or canola oil
4 large eggs
1 teaspoon pure vanilla extract
Marshmallow Filling (page 155)
Chocolate Glaze (page 146)

VARIATION:

Chocolate Strawberry Bundt Cake Prepare the cake and bake as directed. Stir 3 tablespoons strawberry preserves into the marshmallow filling. Tint as desired with red food coloring. Split and fill as directed, then glaze with Chocolate Glaze as directed. Garnish with fresh strawberries.

1. Preheat the oven to 350°F. Spray a 12-cup Bundt pan with nonstick baking spray with flour.
2. In a large bowl using a handheld mixer, blend together the cake mix, pudding mix, sour cream, milk, oil, eggs, and vanilla on low speed. Scrape down the sides of the bowl well and beat on medium speed for 2 minutes.
3. Pour the batter into the prepared pan. Bake for 40 to 50 minutes, or until a wooden pick inserted into the center comes out clean.
4. Place the cake on a wire rack to cool for 10 minutes. Invert the cake onto the rack and let cool completely.
5. Using a serrated knife, slice the cake in half horizontally, making two layers. Place the bottom half on a serving platter. Spread the Marshmallow Filling over the first cake layer. Place the second layer over the filling, cut-side down. Drizzle the Chocolate Glaze evenly over the entire cake.
6. Store the cake in the refrigerator until ready to serve. Keep any leftovers refrigerated.

Chocolate Tuxedo Bundt Cake

MAKES 1 BUNDT CAKE

The stylish and elegant black tuxedo is always impressive, and the events where you see it worn are memorable. Can you picture that smart black jacket with just a glimpse of the formal white shirt beneath? That is the inspiration for this sophisticated Chocolate Tuxedo Bundt Cake. Slice a piece, and you will find rich chocolate cake with a band of vanilla cake through the center. Add the elegant chocolate ganache and a drizzle of white chocolate, and you have a classy, delicious cake that is ideal for any special event.

Nonstick baking spray with flour

¾ cup unsweetened cocoa powder

⅓ cup packed brown sugar

1 teaspoon instant espresso powder

½ cup boiling water

2⅓ cups all-purpose flour

1½ teaspoons baking powder

½ teaspoon baking soda

½ teaspoon salt

1½ cups (3 sticks) unsalted butter, softened

2 cups granulated sugar

6 large eggs

2 teaspoons pure vanilla extract

¾ cup plus 2 tablespoons whole milk

Chocolate Ganache (page 147)

3 ounces white chocolate, chopped

2 tablespoons heavy cream

TIPS:

To create a fun "tuxedo-like" look, drizzle a stripe of white chocolate, about 1 inch wide, from the center of the cake, up over the top, and all the way down to the plate. (Do this before drizzling the cake with the Chocolate Ganache.) Repeat with a second identical stripe, directly across the cake from the first stripe. Spoon the Chocolate Ganache over the rest of the cake, coming close to, but not over, the white stripes.

If desired, alternately spoon the chocolate and vanilla cake batters into the prepared pan and swirl to create a marbled effect. Bake as directed.

1. Preheat the oven to 350°F. Spray a 12-cup Bundt pan with nonstick baking spray with flour.
2. In a small bowl, whisk together the cocoa powder, brown sugar, espresso powder, and boiling water. Whisk until smooth and blended. Set aside to cool completely.
3. In a medium bowl, whisk together the flour, baking powder, baking soda, and salt; set aside.

4. In a large bowl using a handheld mixer, beat together the butter and granulated sugar on medium-high speed for 3 to 5 minutes, or until light and fluffy. Beat in the eggs one at a time, beating well after each addition. Beat in the vanilla.

5. With the mixer on low speed, beat in the flour mixture in three additions, alternating with ¾ cup of the milk, beginning and ending with the flour.

6. Spoon 2 cups of the vanilla batter into a small bowl. Stir in the remaining 2 tablespoons milk; set aside.

7. Pour the chocolate mixture into the remaining batter in the large bowl. Beat on medium speed until blended and smooth.

8. Spoon half the chocolate batter into the prepared pan. Smooth the batter into an even layer. Spoon the vanilla batter over the chocolate batter in the pan and gently smooth it into an even layer. Spoon the remaining chocolate batter over the vanilla layer and gently smooth it into an even layer. Do not blend the layers together.

9. Bake for 50 to 60 minutes, or until a wooden pick inserted into the center comes out clean.

10. Place the cake on a wire rack to cool for 10 minutes. Invert the cake onto the rack and let cool completely.

11. Set the cake on the rack over a sheet of parchment paper to catch any drips and drizzle with the Chocolate Ganache. Refrigerate the cake for about 1 hour so the ganache cools and firms slightly.

12. In a small microwave-safe glass bowl, microwave the white chocolate and the heavy cream on High (100%) power for 30 seconds or just until the cream begins to boil. Stir until the white chocolate has melted and the mixture is smooth. Spoon the melted white chocolate into a small zip-top bag and snip off a small corner of the bag. Drizzle thin stripes of white chocolate in a decorative fashion over the Chocolate Ganache.

A YEAR OF BUNDTS

January: Champagne Celebration Bundt Cake

MAKES 1 BUNDT CAKE

It is time to toast the New Year! Invite your friends to the celebration as you look forward to the year ahead. A treat that is definitely a must on any party menu is this Champagne Celebration Bundt Cake. Just pop the champagne and save a little to make the glaze for the cake.

Nonstick baking spray with flour

3 cups all-purpose flour

2 teaspoons baking powder

½ teaspoon baking soda

½ teaspoon salt

¾ cup (1½ sticks) unsalted butter, softened

2 cups granulated sugar

5 large eggs

2 teaspoons pure vanilla extract

3 to 5 drops red food coloring

1½ cups Champagne (preferably a Brut), at room temperature

Champagne Glaze (page 151)

TIPS:

If you prefer, substitute ginger ale for the champagne.

For a decorative presentation, pipe the glaze in stripes using a pastry bag or a zip-top bag with one corner snipped off. Pipe stripes of glaze from the center of the cake, across the top, and down the side.

1. Preheat the oven to 325°F. Spray a 12-cup Bundt pan with the nonstick baking spray with flour.
2. In a medium bowl, whisk together the flour, baking powder, baking soda, and salt; set aside.
3. In a large bowl using a handheld mixer, beat together the butter and sugar on medium-high speed for 3 to 5 minutes, or until light and fluffy. Beat in the eggs one at a time, beating well after each addition. Beat in the vanilla and the red food coloring.
4. With the mixer on low speed, beat in the flour mixture in three additions, alternating with the champagne, beginning and ending with the flour.
5. Pour the batter into the prepared pan. Bake for 40 to 50 minutes or until a wooden pick inserted into the center comes out clean.
6. Place the cake on a wire rack to cool for 10 minutes. Invert the cake onto the rack and let cool completely.
7. Set the cake on the rack over a sheet of parchment paper to catch any drips and drizzle with the champagne Glaze.

February: Chock-Full of Cherries Bundt Cake

MAKES 1 BUNDT CAKE

Do you love cherry pecan as much as Roxanne does? It is a great flavor combo, and we are always searching for sweet treats, including ice cream, cookies, and cakes, that contain both cherries and pecans. Therefore, we present to you this Chock-Full of Cherries Bundt Cake. You will thank us. It begins with canned dark, sweet cherries so you can enjoy it all year long. Now think of moist, wonderful cake studded with dark red gems and the crunch of pecans. Oh, wow!

Nonstick baking spray with flour

1 (15-ounce) can dark sweet cherries, drained, syrup reserved and cherries cut into quarters

1 (15.25- to 18-ounce) box vanilla or white cake mix

1 (3.4-ounce) box vanilla instant pudding mix

4 large eggs

½ cup water

½ cup vegetable or canola oil

½ teaspoon almond extract

¼ teaspoon red food coloring

½ cup chopped pecans, toasted (see page 12)

Dark Sweet Cherry Glaze

1½ cups confectioners' sugar

1 to 2 tablespoons whole milk

½ teaspoon almond extract

3 or 4 drops red food coloring

TIP:

Dark sweet cherries are deep burgundy in color. Tint the batter and the glaze with red food coloring if you want a brighter red color. Omit the food coloring if you prefer the darker color.

1. Preheat the oven to 350°F. Spray a 12-cup Bundt pan with nonstick baking spray with flour.
2. Drain the cut cherries on a paper towel, then pat dry with clean paper towels. In a small bowl, toss together the chopped cherries and 2 tablespoons of the dry cake mix; set aside.

3. In a large bowl using a handheld mixer, blend together the remaining cake mix, the vanilla pudding mix, ¼ cup of the reserved cherry syrup (reserve remaining syrup for the glaze), the eggs, water, oil, almond extract, and red food coloring on low speed. Scrape down the sides of the bowl well and beat on medium speed for 2 minutes. Stir in the chopped cherry mixture and the pecans.

4. Spoon the batter into the prepared pan. Bake for 40 to 50 minutes, or until a wooden pick inserted into the center comes out clean.

5. Place the cake on a wire rack to cool for 10 minutes. Invert the cake onto the rack and let cool completely.

6. Meanwhile, make the Dark Sweet Cherry Glaze: In a small bowl, whisk together the confectioners' sugar, 1½ tablespoons of the reserved cherry syrup, the milk, almond extract, and red food coloring until smooth.

7. Set the cake on the rack over a sheet of parchment paper to catch any drips and drizzle with the Dark Sweet Cherry Glaze.

March: King Cake Bundt

MAKES 1 BUNDT CAKE

Roxanne looks forward to hosting a Mardi Gras party every year. Beads, jambalaya, and King Cake are a must at these parties. King Cake appears during the religious celebration of Epiphany on January 6 of each year. King Cake is served until Ash Wednesday and the beginning of Lent, and traditionally has a small oven-safe baby trinket or a bean hidden in the batter. Whoever finds the trinket is king for the day and gets to host the next party. Since Roxanne is busy planning the party, she adores baking this streamlined version of the classic.

Nonstick baking spray with flour
½ cup packed brown sugar
2 tablespoons all-purpose flour
½ cup chopped pecans, toasted (see page 12)
1½ teaspoons ground cinnamon
1 (15.25- to 18-ounce) box yellow cake mix
3 large eggs
½ cup sour cream
½ cup vegetable or canola oil
⅓ cup water
1 oven-safe Mardi Gras baby trinket or a dry bean
Almond Glaze (page 142)
Green, yellow, and purple sparkling sugar, for garnish

1. Preheat the oven to 350°F. Spray a 10-cup Bundt pan with nonstick baking spray with flour.
2. In a small bowl, stir together the brown sugar, flour, pecans, and cinnamon; set aside.
3. In a large bowl using a handheld mixer, blend together the cake mix, eggs, sour cream, oil, and water on low speed. Scrape down the sides of the bowl well and beat on medium speed for 2 minutes.
4. Pour half the batter into the prepared pan. Sprinkle the cinnamon-pecan mixture over the batter. Pour the remaining batter on top. Place the trinket in the batter and use a skewer to poke it farther down into the batter. Make sure the trinket is in the middle of the batter and does not touch the sides or bottom of the pan.

5. Bake for 35 to 45 minutes, or until a wooden pick inserted into the center comes out clean.
6. Place the cake on a wire rack to cool for 10 minutes. Invert the cake onto the rack and let cool completely.
7. Set the cake on the rack over a sheet of parchment paper to catch any drips and drizzle with the Almond Glaze. Sprinkle wide bands of the colored sparkling sugars over the cake, alternating colors.

April: Glazed Lemon Bundt Cake

MAKES 1 BUNDT CAKE

We are blessed to have a strong support team of food professionals in Kansas City. Judith Fertig, a cookbook author and novelist, developed a lemon sheet cake for her book All-American Desserts. *We adapted this tasty recipe for a Bundt pan, and we think you will agree that it is delicious. Thanks, Judith, for sharing your recipe and for your continued support.*

Nonstick baking spray with flour
1 (15.25- to 18-ounce) box lemon cake mix
1 (3.4-ounce) box lemon instant pudding mix
Grated zest and juice of 1 lemon
4 large eggs
1 cup water
⅓ cup vegetable or canola oil
Lemon Glaze (page 144)

TIP:

If fresh lemons are not available, substitute 2 tablespoons bottled lemon juice and omit the lemon zest.

1. Preheat the oven to 350°F. Spray a 10-cup Bundt pan with nonstick baking spray with flour.
2. In a large bowl using a handheld mixer, blend together the cake mix, pudding mix, lemon zest, lemon juice, eggs, water, and oil on low speed. Scrape down the sides of the bowl well and beat on medium speed for 2 minutes.
3. Pour the batter into the prepared pan. Bake for 35 to 45 minutes, or until a wooden pick inserted into the center comes out clean.
4. Place the cake on a wire rack to cool for 10 minutes. Invert the cake onto the rack and set the rack over a piece of parchment paper to catch any drips.
5. While the cake is still warm, prepare the Lemon Glaze. Use a skewer to poke holes into the cake. Drizzle the Lemon Glaze over the cake.

May: Kentucky Derby Mint Julep Bundt Cake

MAKES 1 BUNDT CAKE

Put on your hat and listen for the sound of the bugle. It is Kentucky Derby time, and if you are not lucky enough to be attending the famed race, you are probably gathering with friends for a fun time predicting the winning horses. The classic drink for the race is the famous Mint Julep, made of mint and good Kentucky bourbon, and those flavors are featured in this irresistible Kentucky Derby Mint Julep Bundt Cake. Serve slices of this dessert, and your derby gathering is sure to be a winning party!

Nonstick baking spray with flour
¼ cup lightly packed mint leaves, very finely minced, plus whole
    leaves for garnish if desired
6 tablespoons bourbon
2 cups all-purpose flour
1 teaspoon baking powder
½ teaspoon baking soda
½ teaspoon salt
⅔ cup (10 ⅔ tablespoons) unsalted butter, softened
1½ cups granulated sugar
4 large eggs
2 teaspoons pure vanilla extract
¾ cup sour cream
Confectioners' Bourbon Glaze (page 142)

1. Preheat the oven to 325°F. Spray a 10-cup Bundt pan with nonstick baking spray with flour.
2. In a small bowl, combine the minced mint and bourbon; set aside.
3. In a medium bowl, whisk together the flour, baking powder, baking soda, and salt; set aside.
4. In a large bowl using a handheld mixer, beat together the butter and granulated sugar on medium speed for 3 to 5 minutes, or until light and fluffy. Beat in the eggs one a time, beating well after each addition. Beat in the vanilla and sour cream.
5. With the mixer on low speed, beat in the flour mixture in three additions, alternating with the mint-bourbon mixture, beginning and ending with the flour.

6. Pour the batter into the prepared pan. Bake for 40 to 50 minutes, or until a wooden pick inserted into the center comes out clean.

7. Place the cake on a wire rack to cool for 10 minutes. Invert the cake onto the rack and let cool completely.

8. Se the cake on the rack over a sheet of parchment paper to catch any drips and drizzle with the Confectioners' Bourbon Glaze. Garnish with fresh mint leaves, if desired.

VARIATIONS:

Mojito Bundt Cake

Substitute rum for the bourbon. Prepare and bake the cake as directed. Glaze with Mojito Glaze (page 142) instead of the Confectioners' Bourbon Glaze.

June: Strawberry Angel Bundt Cake

MAKES 1 BUNDT CAKE

Who knew you could bake angel food cake in a Bundt pan rather than a tube pan? An angel food cake baked in a Bundt pan makes everything taste better. Add strawberries and cream to the mix, and you have an elegant dessert for any dinner party menu.

1 (16-ounce) box angel food cake mix
Water, as directed on the cake mix box

Strawberry Cream Filling

1½ cups coarsely chopped fresh strawberries
2 cups heavy cream
3 tablespoons confectioners' sugar
5 or 6 whole strawberries, stemmed and halved

1. Preheat the oven as directed on the cake mix box.
2. Prepare the angel food cake batter according to the package directions. Spoon the batter into a 10-cup Bundt pan that has *not* been sprayed with nonstick spray. Bake according to the package directions.
3. Invert the cake in the pan onto a glass bottle (a wine bottle works well for this) and let cool for 1½ hours.
4. Meanwhile, make the Strawberry Cream Filling: Place the chopped strawberries in a medium bowl; set aside.
5. In a separate medium bowl using a handheld mixer, beat together the cream and confectioners' sugar on medium speed. Increase the speed to medium-high and beat until the cream holds stiff peaks. Spoon half the whipped cream into the bowl with the strawberries. Fold the strawberries and whipped cream together.
6. Carefully run a butter knife or flat metal spatula around the sides of the cooled cake. Remove the cake from the pan. Using a serrated knife, cut the cake in half horizontally to make two layers. Set one layer on a serving platter, cut-side up. Spread the Strawberry Cream Filling over the cut side of the first cake layer. Top with the second cake layer, cut-side down. Spread the remaining whipped cream over the top and, if you can, down the sides slightly. Garnish the top with strawberry halves.

TIPS:

This is wonderful prepared with a medley of berries, such as strawberries, blueberries and raspberries.

Substitute 1 (8- to 12-ounce) tub frozen whipped topping, thawed, for the heavy cream. Do not whip. Stir the berries into half the whipped topping and fill the cake as directed. Frost the top of the cake with the remaining whipped topping. Garnish with strawberry halves as directed.

Store the cake in the refrigerator until ready to serve. Keep any leftovers refrigerated.

July: Vanilla Raspberry Swirl Bundt Cake

MAKES 1 BUNDT CAKE

Don't you love it when something you bake looks gorgeous, yet you really (honestly) did not do anything special? That is so true for this Vanilla Raspberry Swirl Bundt Cake. The ruby red swirl contrasts beautifully with the white vanilla cake, so when you put that slice on a plate, you will have a dessert readymade for an Instagram or Pinterest photo, and the flavor is just as good.

Nonstick baking spray with flour
1 (15.25- to 18-ounce) box vanilla or white cake mix
1 (3.4-ounce) box vanilla instant pudding mix
2 teaspoons pure vanilla extract
½ cup (1 stick) unsalted butter, melted
4 large eggs
1 cup buttermilk
Vanilla Glaze (page 142)
Fresh raspberries, for garnish (optional)

Raspberry Swirl Filling

¼ cup granulated sugar
1 tablespoon cornstarch
6 tablespoons water
1 cup frozen raspberries, thawed, juice reserved

TIPS:

If you want a seedless raspberry swirl, pour the hot Raspberry Swirl Filling through a sieve to remove the seeds, then allow the filling to cool completely.

If fresh raspberries are in season, substitute them for the frozen berries and cook as directed to make the Raspberry Swirl Filling.

1. Preheat the oven to 350°F. Spray a 12-cup Bundt pan with nonstick baking spray with flour.
2. Make the Raspberry Swirl Filling: In a small saucepan, mix together the sugar and cornstarch. Stir in the water until blended. Stir in the raspberries and any collected juice. Cook over medium heat, stirring continuously, until the mixture is bubbling and thickened, about 5 minutes. Set aside to cool completely.
3. In a large bowl using a handheld mixer, blend together the cake mix, pudding mix, vanilla, melted butter, eggs, and buttermilk on low speed. Scrape down the sides of the bowl well and beat on medium speed for 2 minutes.

4. Pour about half the vanilla batter into the prepared pan. Dollop about half the Raspberry Swirl Filling evenly over the batter in the pan. Top with the remaining vanilla batter and dollop with the remaining Raspberry Swirl Filling. Gently draw a butter knife through the batter to create a marbled effect (do not overblend—the batter and the filling should remain distinct).

5. Bake for 45 to 55 minutes, or until the cake begins to pull away from the sides of the pan and the center springs back when touched lightly. (You cannot test for doneness with a wooden pick as the cake has a raspberry filling.)

6. Place the cake on a wire rack to cool for 10 minutes. Invert the cake onto the rack and let cool completely.

7. Set the cake on the rack over a sheet of parchment paper to catch any drips and drizzle with the Vanilla Glaze. Garnish with fresh raspberries, if desired.

VARIATIONS:

Chocolate Raspberry Swirl Bundt Cake

Substitute devil's food cake mix for the vanilla cake mix and chocolate instant pudding mix for the vanilla instant pudding. Prepare the cake with the Raspberry Swirl as directed, then bake as directed. Glaze with Chocolate Ganache (page 147) instead of Vanilla Glaze and garnish with fresh raspberries.

August: Peanut Butter and Jelly Bundt Cake

MAKES 1 BUNDT CAKE

Peanut butter and jelly seem to have been married since the beginning of time, and why not? The combination is delightful and begs for a cold glass of milk. This is fun to make anytime, but especially on the first day of school. What better way to guarantee the school year is off to a grand start?

Nonstick baking spray with flour
1 (15.25- to 18-ounce) box yellow cake mix
½ cup water
½ cup whole milk
½ cup vegetable or canola oil
⅓ cup creamy peanut butter
4 large eggs
1 teaspoon pure vanilla extract
½ cup grape, strawberry, or raspberry jelly
Peanut Butter Glaze (page 155)

TIP:

Sprinkle the glaze with about ⅓ cup coarsely chopped dry-roasted peanuts, if desired.

1. Preheat the oven to 350°F. Spray a 10-cup Bundt pan with nonstick baking spray with flour.
2. In a large bowl using a handheld mixer, blend together the cake mix, water, milk, oil, peanut butter, eggs, and vanilla on low speed. Scrape down the sides of the bowl well and beat on medium speed for 2 minutes.
3. Pour the batter into the prepared pan. Bake for 35 to 45 minutes, or until a wooden pick inserted into the center comes out clean.
4. Place the cake on a wire rack to cool for 10 minutes. Invert the cake onto the rack and let cool completely.
5. Use a serrated knife to slice the Bundt cake in half horizontally, making two layers. Place one layer on a serving plate, cut-side up.
6. In a small microwave-safe glass bowl, microwave the jelly on High (100%) power for 30 seconds. Stir until smooth. Spread the jelly evenly over the cut side of the first cake layer. Top with the second cake layer, cut-side down. Drizzle with the Peanut Butter Glaze.

VARIATIONS:

Chocolate Peanut Butter Bundt Cake

Prepare and bake the cake as directed. Do not split and fill the cake. Drizzle with Chocolate Glaze (page 146). Garnish with chopped peanut butter cup candies.

September: Caramel Apple Bundt Cake

MAKES 1 BUNDT CAKE

It just doesn't seem to be fall without dipping apples in sweet caramel. For many of us, it is such an amazing flavor combo that it is hard to wait until the autumn months. With this Caramel Apple Bundt Cake, you can easily enjoy that flavor any time you want. Diced apples in a moist cake, topped with rich caramel and a sprinkling of pecans capture all those timeless flavors. Don't wait to make this scrumptious cake.

Nonstick baking spray with flour

1 large tart apple, such as a Granny Smith, peeled, cored, and very finely chopped

1 (15.25- to 18-ounce) box yellow cake mix

1 (3.4-ounce) box butterscotch instant pudding mix

4 large eggs

1⅓ cups applesauce

½ cup (1 stick) unsalted butter, melted

1½ teaspoons pumpkin pie spice

¾ cup caramel ice cream topping (see Tip, page 55)

½ cup chopped pecans, toasted (see page 12)

TIP:

If desired, top the cake with ½ recipe Caramel Icing (page 150) instead of the caramel topping.

1. Preheat the oven to 350°F. Spray a 12-cup Bundt pan with nonstick baking spray with flour.
2. In a small bowl, toss together the apple and 2 tablespoons of the dry cake mix; set aside.
3. In a large bowl using a handheld mixer, blend together the remaining cake mix, the pudding mix, eggs, applesauce, melted butter, and pumpkin pie spice on low speed. Scrape down the sides of the bowl well and beat on medium speed for 2 minutes. Stir in the apple mixture by hand.
4. Spoon the batter into the prepared pan. Bake for 45 to 55 minutes, or until a wooden pick inserted into the center comes out clean.
5. Place the cake on a wire rack to cool for 10 minutes. Invert the cake onto the rack and let cool completely.
6. Set the cake on the rack over a sheet of parchment paper to catch any drips and drizzle with the caramel topping. Sprinkle with the chopped pecans.

October: Gingerbread Bundt Cake

MAKES 1 BUNDT CAKE

Gingerbread cake has truly become an American classic, with roots that run deep into our European heritage. Thank goodness the English, French, and Germans all brought versions of gingerbread to America. This Gingerbread Bundt Cake recipe is stirred together in minutes and bakes into a spice-filled cake that will definitely become a keeper in your recipe box.

Nonstick baking spray with flour
2¾ cups all-purpose flour
½ teaspoon baking powder
½ teaspoon baking soda
½ teaspoon salt
2 teaspoons ground ginger
1½ teaspoons ground cinnamon
½ teaspoon ground nutmeg
½ teaspoon ground cloves
¼ teaspoon ground allspice
4 large eggs
1½ cups packed brown sugar
1 cup (2 sticks) unsalted butter, melted
1 cup sour cream
½ cup molasses
Sweetened whipped cream, for serving

TIPS:

This recipe spice blend is one we like. It does require quite a few spices to attain the gingerbread flavor; that said, if you do not have allspice on hand, it can be omitted.

When measuring molasses, or any sticky ingredient, first spray the measuring cup with nonstick cooking spray. It will make it much easier to get all the molasses out of the cup.

If desired, sift confectioners' sugar over the cake just before serving.

Slice and top each slice with a large dollop of whipped cream.

1. Preheat the oven to 350°F. Spray a 10-cup Bundt pan with nonstick baking spray with flour.
2. In a medium bowl, whisk together the flour, baking powder, baking soda, salt, ginger, cinnamon, nutmeg, cloves, and allspice; set aside.
3. In a large bowl, whisk the eggs. Add the brown sugar and whisk until combined. Add the melted butter, sour cream, and molasses; stir to combine. Gently stir in the flour mixture until blended.
4. Pour the batter into the prepared pan. Bake for 45 to 55 minutes, or until a wooden pick inserted into the center comes out clean.
5. Place the cake on a wire rack to cool for 10 minutes. Invert the cake onto the rack. The cake can be served warm or at room temperature.

November: Cranberry-Orange Bundt Cake

MAKES 1 BUNDT CAKE

No need to wait for the holidays to enjoy this jewel-studded cake. This Cranberry-Orange Bundt Cake recipe rivals the local bakery's version any day! We always tell students at our cooking classes to purchase cranberries when they are in season and freeze them for use throughout the year.

Nonstick baking spray with flour

1 (15.25- to 18-ounce) box yellow cake mix

1 cup orange juice

½ cup vegetable or canola oil

⅓ cup granulated sugar

4 large eggs

1 cup fresh cranberries

1 tablespoon all-purpose flour

Quick Orange Glaze (page **144**)

1. Preheat the oven to 350°F. Spray a 10-cup Bundt pan with nonstick baking spray with flour.
2. In a large bowl using a handheld mixer, beat together the cake mix, orange juice, oil, sugar, and eggs on low speed. Scrape down the sides of the bowl well and beat on medium speed for 2 minutes.
3. In a small bowl or a zip-top bag, toss the cranberries with the flour to coat evenly. Stir the cranberries into the cake batter.
4. Pour the batter into the prepared pan. Bake for 35 to 45 minutes, or until a wooden pick inserted into the center comes out clean.
5. Place the cake on a wire rack to cool for 10 minutes. Invert the cake onto the rack and let cool completely.
6. Set the cake on the rack over a sheet of parchment paper to catch any drips and drizzle with the Quick Orange Glaze.

VARIATION:

Blueberry-Orange Bundt Cake Substitute fresh or frozen (not thawed) blueberries for the cranberries. Prepare and bake the cake as directed. Glaze with Quick Orange Glaze as directed.

TIP:

Frozen cranberries can be substituted for the fresh cranberries. Thaw them and pat dry, then toss with the flour as directed in the recipe.

December: Peppermint Candy Cane Bundt Cake

MAKES 1 BUNDT CAKE

Swirls of peppermint can only mean one thing: it is holiday time, and candy canes are every-where. This Peppermint Candy Cane Bundt Cake is just as pretty as it is tasty, so it can be the centerpiece of your holiday meal.

Nonstick baking spray with flour
1 (15.25- to 18-ounce) box vanilla or white cake mix
1 (3.4-ounce) box vanilla instant pudding mix
4 large eggs
¾ cup whole milk
½ cup vegetable or canola oil
1 teaspoon peppermint extract
¾ teaspoon red food coloring
Vanilla Glaze (page 142)
¼ cup crushed peppermint candy (about 3 candy canes or 12 mints)

1. Preheat the oven to 350°F. Spray a 12-cup Bundt pan with nonstick baking spray with flour.
2. In a large bowl using a handheld mixer, blend together the cake mix, pudding mix, eggs, milk, and oil on low speed. Scrape down the sides of the bowl well and beat on medium speed for 2 minutes.
3. Spoon 2 cups of the batter into a small bowl and set aside.
4. Stir the peppermint extract and red food coloring into the remaining batter.
5. Alternately spoon the peppermint batter and vanilla batter into the prepared pan. Gently draw a butter knife through the batter to create a marbled effect (do not overblend—the peppermint and vanilla batters should remain distinct).
6. Bake for 35 to 45 minutes, or until a wooden pick inserted into the center comes out clean.
7. Place the cake on a wire rack to cool for 10 minutes. Invert the cake onto the rack and let cool completely.
8. Set the cake on the rack over a sheet of parchment paper to catch any drips and drizzle with the Vanilla Glaze. Immediately sprinkle with the crushed peppermint candy.

GLAZES, FROSTINGS, AND FILLINGS

GLAZE AND FROSTING TIPS

In the cake recipes, we suggest some of our favorite cake and glaze combinations, but you are welcome to mix and match the flavors of the glazes and frostings with the cakes as you prefer.

Some people like glazes thin and pourable, while others prefer a thicker or firmer glaze. Choose the thickness you prefer. If a thinner or softer glaze is desired, blend in a little more liquid, a teaspoon at a time, until the desired consistency is reached. If a thicker or firmer glaze is preferred, blend in additional confectioners' sugar, 1 to 2 tablespoons at a time, until the desired consistency is reached.

If the confectioners' sugar appears lumpy as you spoon it out of the package, you may want to sift it before blending it with the liquids. To quickly and easily sift confectioners' sugar, pour it through a sieve and tap the sides gently.

Vanilla Glaze

MAKES ABOUT 1 CUP

2½ cups confectioners' sugar
3 tablespoons whole milk, plus more if needed
1 teaspoon pure vanilla extract

1. In a small bowl, whisk together the confectioners' sugar, milk, and vanilla until smooth.
2. If needed to thin the glaze to a drizzleable consistency, whisk in an additional 1 teaspoon milk.

VARIATIONS:

Almond Glaze: Substitute ½ teaspoon almond extract for the vanilla.

Confectioners' Bourbon Glaze: Substitute 1 tablespoon bourbon for 1 tablespoon of the milk. Blend in the bourbon and the remaining 2 tablespoons of milk, or as needed until it is the desired consistency.

Mojito Glaze: Substitute 1 tablespoon rum for 1 tablespoon of the milk. Blend in the rum and the remaining 2 tablespoons of milk, or as needed until it is the desired consistency.

Pineapple Glaze: Substitute pineapple juice for the milk.

Cream Cheese Glaze

MAKES ABOUT 1 CUP

4 ounces cream cheese, softened
1 cup confectioners' sugar, sifted
½ teaspoon pure vanilla extract
2 to 3 tablespoons whole milk

In a medium bowl using a handheld mixer, beat together the cream cheese, confectioners' sugar, and vanilla on medium speed. Add the milk as needed to reach the desired consistency. This glaze should be thick but pourable.

Rich Cream Glaze

MAKES ABOUT ½ CUP

1¼ cups confectioners' sugar
¼ cup heavy cream
½ teaspoon pure vanilla extract

In a small bowl, whisk together the confectioners' sugar, cream, and vanilla until smooth.

Lemon Glaze

MAKES ABOUT 1¼ CUPS

  3 cups confectioners' sugar, sifted
  ⅓ cup fresh lemon juice

In a small bowl, whisk together confectioners' sugar and lemon juice until smooth.

TIP:

We prefer fresh lemon juice, but in a pinch you could use bottled lemon juice.

Quick Orange Glaze

MAKES ABOUT ⅓ CUP

  1 cup confectioners' sugar
  2 tablespoons orange juice

In a small bowl, whisk together the confectioners' sugar and orange juice until smooth.

Orange Glaze

MAKES ABOUT 1 CUP PLUS 2 TABLESPOONS

1 cup orange juice
1 cup confectioners' sugar
1 teaspoon pure vanilla extract

In a small saucepan, combine the orange juice, confectioners' sugar, and vanilla. Bring to a boil over medium-high heat, stirring occasionally. Remove from the heat and allow to cool for 30 minutes before using.

Bourbon Glaze

MAKES ABOUT ¾ CUP

⅓ cup (5⅓ tablespoons) unsalted butter, cut into cubes
¾ cup granulated sugar
¼ cup bourbon

In a small saucepan, combine the butter, sugar, and bourbon. Bring to a boil over medium-high heat, stirring frequently. Boil for 2 minutes, or until the sugar has dissolved. Remove from the heat and allow to stand for 5 minutes. If the mixture starts to set too much before you're ready to use it, gently reheat it over low heat.

VARIATIONS:

Apple Cider Glaze: Substitute apple cider for the bourbon. Proceed as recipe directions indicate.

Chocolate Glaze

MAKES ABOUT ¾ CUP

1 cup semisweet chocolate chips
¼ cup (½ stick) unsalted butter
2 tablespoons light corn syrup

In a medium microwave-safe glass bowl, microwave the chocolate chips, butter, and corn syrup on High (100%) power for 1 minute. Remove from the microwave and stir until smooth. If needed, continue to microwave in 30-second intervals on High (100%) power until melted and smooth.

Chocolate Frosting

MAKES ABOUT 2 CUPS

6 tablespoons (¾ stick) unsalted butter
¼ cup unsweetened cocoa powder
¼ cup whole milk
2¾ cups confectioners' sugar

TIP:

If the confectioners' sugar appears lumpy, sift it before adding it to the chocolate mixture.

In a medium saucepan, melt the butter over medium heat. Add the cocoa powder and milk and stir well. Bring to a boil and boil for 1 minute, stirring continuously. Remove from the heat. Whisk in the confectioners' sugar. Continue to whisk for 2 to 3 minutes, or until the frosting is thick, smooth, and the desired consistency.

Chocolate-Mint Glaze

MAKES ABOUT ¾ CUP

1 cup semisweet chocolate chips
⅓ cup heavy cream
½ teaspoon peppermint extract

In a microwave-safe 1-cup glass measuring cup or bowl, microwave the chocolate chips and the cream on High (100%) power for 30 seconds; stir until smooth. If needed, microwave on High (100%) power for 15 seconds more or until the chocolate chips are melted. Stir in the peppermint extract until smooth.

VARIATION:

Milk Chocolate Glaze
Prepare the glaze as directed, using milk chocolate chips instead of semisweet. Omit the peppermint extract and blend in ½ teaspoon pure vanilla extract.

Chocolate Ganache

MAKES ABOUT ¾ CUP

½ cup semisweet chocolate chips
¼ cup heavy cream
2 tablespoons unsalted butter
½ teaspoon pure vanilla extract
2 teaspoons confectioners' sugar

1. Place the semisweet chips in a small bowl; set aside.
2. In a microwave-safe 1-cup glass measuring cup or bowl, microwave the cream and butter on High (100%) power for 25 to 35 seconds, or until the cream is hot and the butter is beginning to melt. Stir to finish melting the butter, if necessary. Pour the hot cream mixture over the semisweet chocolate chips. Using a small whisk, whisk until smooth. Add the vanilla and confectioners' sugar and continue whisking until smooth.

White Chocolate Glaze

MAKES ABOUT ⅓ CUP

1 (4-ounce) bar white chocolate, chopped
1 tablespoon confectioners' sugar
1 tablespoon plus 2 teaspoons whole milk

In a small microwave-safe glass bowl, microwave the white chocolate on High (100%) power in 20-second intervals, stirring after each, until melted and smooth. (Watch carefully to avoid scorching and stir after each interval to avoid overheating the chocolate.) Add the confectioners' sugar and milk. Stir until smooth.

Pomegranate Glaze

MAKES ABOUT ½ CUP

1⅓ cups confectioners' sugar
2 tablespoons unsweetened pomegranate juice
1 tablespoon fresh lemon juice

In a small bowl, whisk together the confectioners' sugar, pomegranate juice, and lemon juice until smooth.

TIP:

Pomegranate juice is available sweetened or unsweetened. We prefer to use unsweetened 100% juice, and our favorite is Pom brand, which is readily found at most grocery stores in the refrigerated case. If you have leftover juice after making this glaze, you can drink the refreshing sweet-tart juice or make it into a smoothie by blending it with yogurt, fresh berries, and, if you prefer it sweeter, a touch of honey.

Caramel Icing

MAKES ABOUT 2 CUPS

36 caramels, unwrapped
1 (14-ounce) can sweetened condensed milk
4 tablespoons (½ stick) unsalted butter, cut into cubes

In a medium saucepan, combine the caramels, sweetened condensed milk, and butter. Heat over medium heat, stirring continuously until the caramels are melted and the mixture is smooth. Allow to cool for 2 to 3 minutes, or until the icing is the desired consistency, stirring occasionally.

TIP:

We like to use chewy caramels. For this recipe, we prefer to use Brach's caramels made with real milk.

Praline Icing

MAKES ABOUT 1½ CUPS

½ cup (1 stick) unsalted butter, cut into pieces
1 cup packed brown sugar
¼ cup whole milk
1 cup confectioners' sugar
1 teaspoon pure vanilla extract

In a medium saucepan, combine the butter, brown sugar, and milk. Bring to a boil over medium-high heat, whisking continuously. Boil for 1 minute, stirring continuously, then remove from the heat and whisk in the confectioners' sugar and vanilla. Continue to stir for at least 5 minutes, or until the mixture is smooth and thickens.

Champagne Glaze

MAKES ABOUT 1 CUP

½ cup (1 stick) butter, softened
2 cups confectioners' sugar
½ teaspoon pure vanilla extract
2 tablespoons champagne
2 or 3 drops red food coloring

In a medium bowl using a handheld mixer, beat together the butter and confectioners' sugar on medium speed until creamy. Add the vanilla, champagne, and food coloring and beat well.

TIPS:

This glaze is a little thicker, so you can pipe it over the Bundt cake in a decorative fashion. If a thinner glaze is desired or you'd like to drizzle it over the cake, blend in additional champagne until the glaze reaches the desired consistency.

If you prefer, substitute ginger ale for the champagne.

Brown Sugar Glaze

MAKES ABOUT ¾ CUP

3 tablespoons unsalted butter
⅓ cup packed brown sugar
Dash of salt
3 tablespoons heavy cream
1 teaspoon pure vanilla extract

In a small saucepan, melt the butter over low heat. Stir in the brown sugar and the salt and cook, stirring, for 1 minute, or until the sugar has dissolved and the mixture is bubbling. Stir in the cream and cook, stirring continuously, for 1 minute. Remove from the heat and stir in the vanilla.

Maple Frosting

3 tablespoons unsalted butter, melted
1 cup confectioners' sugar
3 to 4 tablespoons pure maple syrup
1 teaspoon pure vanilla extract

In a small bowl, whisk together the melted butter, confectioners' sugar, maple syrup, and vanilla until smooth.

TIP:

If you don't have syrup, you can substitute milk for the maple syrup and add ½ teaspoon maple extract. Proceed as directed.

Cola Icing

MAKES ABOUT 2 CUPS

½ cup (1 stick) unsalted butter, cut into cubes
⅓ cup cola
¼ cup unsweetened cocoa powder
3 cups confectioners' sugar

In a medium saucepan, combine the butter, cola, and cocoa powder. Bring to a boil over medium-high heat, stirring frequently. Remove from the heat and whisk in the confectioners' sugar. Whisk vigorously until the icing is smooth and shiny.

VARIATIONS:

Cherry Cola Icing: Substitute cherry flavored cola for the regular cola.

Peanut Butter Glaze

MAKES ABOUT ½ CUP

4 tablespoons (½ stick) unsalted butter, melted
3 tablespoons creamy peanut butter
2 to 3 tablespoons confectioners' sugar

In a medium bowl using a handheld mixer, beat together the melted butter, peanut butter, and 2 tablespoons of the confectioners' sugar on high speed. If needed, beat in the additional 1 tablespoon confectioners' sugar to thicken the glaze.

Marshmallow Filling

MAKES ABOUT 2 CUPS

¾ cup (1½ sticks) unsalted butter, softened
1 (7-ounce) jar marshmallow crème
1 teaspoon pure vanilla extract
2 cups confectioners' sugar

In a large bowl using a handheld mixer, beat together the butter, marshmallow crème, and vanilla on medium speed until smooth. Add the confectioners' sugar and beat until smooth.

Acknowledgments

ROXANNE'S FAMILY: A Bundt cake represents a perfect circle, which is exactly what I have been blessed with—a perfect family that completes my circle. To my husband, Bob Bateman, and daughter, Grace: Thank you for your encouragement, love, and devotion with all my kitchen projects, and especially for your help with these Bundt cake recipes. You cheerfully tasted, evaluated, and even helped with dishes! I also want to thank my mom, Colleen Wyss, who instilled in me a love of all things baked.

KATHY'S FAMILY: Words cannot express what my family means to me. My husband, David, and daughters, Laura and Amanda, help me discover how sweet life and love can be. Thank you for days of laughter, for endless trips to the grocery store, and for your patience as I once again escape to my office to write down another recipe. Life would not be complete without each of you.

We are grateful for the incredible team who came together to create this book.

We so appreciate our editors at St. Martin's Press, BJ Berti and Laura Apperson, and want to thank them for their creativity, knowledge, and guidance. The entire St. Martin's team is unsurpassed, and we appreciate all they do to create such beautiful cookbooks.

Working with the Lisa Ekus Group has been a dream come true! It is an amazing team and we truly appreciate Lisa Ekus, Sally Ekus, and every single person in the group who works so hard on our behalf. We cannot thank each of them enough for their friendship and guidance! Thank you.

Staci Valentine and her beautiful photographs add so much to the book and make each recipe come alive. Thank you, Staci, and food stylist Alyse Sakai, for all your hard work.

Thank you to Nordic Ware, for your quality bakeware and continuing support. We also appreciate Lodge Manufacturing Company for sharing a sample of their cast-iron fluted cake pan with us.

We always remember how blessed we are to work together and share such a lasting friendship. Our friendship has been a true lifelong blessing.

And we want to thank you, our avid readers and friends, who prepare our recipes for your families and friends. Please continue to share food and family times with us at www.pluggedintocooking.com.

Index

Mojito Glaze, 142

nuts
  toasting, 12
  see also almond; pecan;
    walnut

oils, 11
Olive Oil-Almond Bundt
  Cake, 32–33
orange
  Citrus Marble Bundt Cake,
    101–2
  Cranberry Bundt Cake, 134,
    135
  Date Nut Bundt Cake, 28–29
  Glaze, 145
  Glaze, Quick, 144
  Sweet Tea Bundt Cake, 36
Overnight Caramel Cinnamon
  Roll Bundt Cake, 86, *87*

peanut butter
  Chocolate Tunnel Bundt
    Cake, *96,* 97–98
  Glaze, 155
  and Jelly Bundt Cake,
    128–29
pecan(s)
  Butter Coffee Cake, 88–89
  Caramel Apple Bundt Cake,
    130, *131*
  Chock-Full of Cherries
    Bundt Cake, 118–19
  Cola Bundt Cake, 64, *65*
  Fudge Brownie Bundt Cake,
    48, *49*
  German Chocolate Bundt
    Cake, 46–47, *47*
  Golden Maple Pound Bundt

Cake, 70
Italian Cream Bundt Cake,
  18, *19*
Kentucky Bourbon Bundt
  Cake, 20
King Cake Bundt, 120–21,
  121
Orange Date Nut Bundt
  Cake, 28–29
Overnight Caramel Cinna-
  mon Roll Bundt Cake, 86,
  87
Snickerdoodle Coffee Cake,
  78, 79
Southern Praline Bundt
  Cake, *16,* 17
toasting, 12
Tomato Soup Spice Bundt
  Cake, *42,* 43
Turtle Bundt Cake, *50,* 51
Watergate Bundt Cake, 22,
  23
peppermint
  Candy Cane Bundt Cake,
    136, 137
  Chocolate-Mint Glaze, 147
  -Glazed Chocolate Bundt
    Cake, 54
pineapple
  Coconut Bundt Cake, 37
  Glaze, 142
  Upside-Down Bundt Cake,
    41
pistachio, Watergate Bundt
  Cake, 22, *23*
Pomegranate Glaze, 148
  White Chocolate Bundt
    Cake with, 56–57, *57*
Poppy Seed-Almond Bundt
  Cake, 38

pound cakes
  Honey Bee Bundt, 76–77
  Sour Cream Chocolate
    Bundt, 72–74, *73*
  Southern Bundt, 70–71
  Spice Bundt, 75
praline
  Bundt Cake, Southern, *16,*
    17
  Icing, 150
Pumpkin Bundt Cake with
  Ginger Swirl, 106–7, *107*

Quick Orange Glaze, 144

rack, wire, 13
raspberry
  Chocolate Bundt Cake, 53
  Vanilla Swirl Bundt Cake,
    126–27
Red Velvet Marble Bundt
  Cake, 94–95, *95*
Rich Cream Glaze, 143
Rosemary-Lemon Bundt
  Cake, 26–27, *27*

salt, 11–12
seasonal Bundt cakes
  January: Champagne Cele-
    bration, *116,* 117
  February: Chock-Full of
    Cherries, 118–19
  March: King Cake, 120–21,
    121
  April: Glazed Lemon, 122
  May: Kentucky Derby Mint
    Julep, 123–24
  June: Strawberry Angel, 125
  July: Vanilla Raspberry
    Swirl, 126–27

August: Peanut Butter and Jelly, 128–29
September: Caramel Apple, 130, *131*
October: Gingerbread, 132, *133*
November: Cranberry-Orange, 134, *135*
December: Peppermint Candy Cane, *136,* 137
shortening, 11
Snickerdoodle Coffee Cake, *78,* 79
sour cream
Bundt Cake, 21
Chocolate Pound Bundt Cake, 72–74, *73*
Southern Pound Bundt Cake, 70–71
Southern Praline Bundt Cake, *16,* 17
Spice Pound Bundt Cake, 75
strawberry
Angel Bundt Cake, 125
Bundt Cake with Balsamic Strawberry Sauce, 34–35,

35
Chocolate Bundt Cake, 109
sugars, 12
Sweet Potato Bundt Cake with Ginger Swirl, 106
Sweet Tea Bundt Cake, 36
swirled Bundt cakes, *see* marble, tunnel, swirled, and filled Bundt cakes

Tea, Sweet, Bundt Cake, 36
Thyme-Zucchini Bundt Cake, 39
Tomato Soup Spice Bundt Cake, *42,* 43
Triple Chocolate Bundt Cake, 52–53
tunnel Bundt cakes, *see* marble, tunnel, swirled, and filled Bundt cakes
Turtle Bundt Cake, *50,* 51

vanilla
Cream Bundt Cake, *92, 93*
Glaze, 142
Raspberry Swirl Bundt

Cake, 126–27
vegetable shortening, 11
walnut(s)
Banana Bundt Coffee Cake, 80–81, *81*
Snickerdoodle Coffee Cake, *78,* 79
toasting, 12
Watergate Bundt Cake, 22, *23*
whipped cream, 12–13
whipped topping, 12
whisk, 13
white chocolate
Bundt Cake with Pomegranate Glaze, 56–57, *57*
Chocolate Tuxedo Bundt Cake, 110–12, *111*
Chocolate Tweed Bundt Cake, 60–61
Glaze, 148
Whoopie Bundt Cake, Chocolate, *108,* 109
wire rack, 13

Zucchini-Thyme Bundt Cake, 39